THE
HISTORY OF THE MAYA

A LINTEL FROM YAXCHILAN

The individual on the right holds in his hands a jaguar's head. Note the tattooing on the cheek, the deformed heads, the armlets, and the long skirt.

THE
HISTORY OF THE MAYA

FROM THE EARLIEST TIMES TO THE
PRESENT DAY

BY

THOMAS GANN, F.R.G.S., F.R.A.I.

IN CHARGE OF RECENT EXPEDITIONS OF THE BRITISH MUSEUM
TO CENTRAL AMERICA

AND

J. ERIC THOMPSON

ASSISTANT CURATOR, FIELD MUSEUM, CHICAGO
LEADER OF THE MARSHALL FIELD EXPEDITIONS TO
CENTRAL AMERICA.

NEW YORK
CHARLES SCRIBNER'S SONS
1937

PREFACE

In this short outline of the Maya civilization the careful reader will detect two or three contradictory statements. The different chapters were written without collaboration. One of the authors wrote his chapters in Belize, British Honduras; the other in Chicago, a couple of thousand miles away. However, apart from the obstacle of distance, it seemed best to leave what each of us had written unamended, as thereby the reader may obtain some insight into the conflicting theories that are held with regard to certain phases of Maya history and religion. Nevertheless, in one case changes have been made for the sake of uniformity. The correlation throughout this book is that advanced by Doctor Herbert J. Spinden. This correlation is favored by Doctor Gann; and Mr. Thompson, who adheres to the 11.16.0.0.0. correlation which makes all Maya dates just short of two hundred and sixty years later, has amended the European dates in his chapter on the history of Yucatan to conform with those used by Doctor Gann in the previous chapter. At the head of each chapter are given the initials of the author responsible for it.

THOMAS GANN,
J. ERIC THOMPSON.

CONTENTS

ILLUSTRATIONS

ILLUSTRATIONS

THE
HISTORY OF THE MAYA

CHAPTER I

ORIGIN OF THE MAYA
(T. G.)

Period at which man first reached the American Continent. His place of origin, and the route by which he arrived. Stratification in the Valley of Mexico, and the light it throws on the development of the aboriginal races. Origin of the Maya. Their long march to Uaxactun. An agricultural people. The development of their civilization. Our sources of information as to their history. Early Spanish Chronicles. The Codices. Native historical records. The Monuments. Oral traditions. Survivals of the ancient traditions and the old religion. Survival of a knowledge of the Maya calendar, to the present day. Maya never completely subdued. Lacondones and Santa Cruz tribes still enjoy a semi-independence.

IT is now generally believed that man first reached the Western Hemisphere in early neolithic times, perhaps 10,000 years ago.

The fact that no implements resembling those made by paleolithic man in the Old World have ever been found in America would go to prove that he had already passed out of the old stone age when this migration took place. On the other hand, the fact that the potter's wheel, the use of metals, domesticated animals, wheeled vehicles, and Old-World cereals, were all unknown to the first discoverers of America, would seem to indicate that they had not as yet emerged from the stone age, and that none of them were acquainted with agriculture, or pastoral pursuits, but that all were

3

still in the nomadic stage of civilization, living on the results of the chase and such wild fruits and roots as were in season.

It appears probable that these early American immigrants came in by way of the Behring Straits, from northeastern Asia, where the continents are separated by less than forty miles of water, bridged during the winter by a solid mass of ice. They must have consisted of bands of various nomadic tribes, all capable of withstanding exposure to an arctic climate, for a considerable period.

The migration lasted probably over several centuries. The tribes differed very much amongst themselves in physical characteristics, and the earlier comers were gradually pushed southward down the continent by the successive waves of migration which followed them. Only in this way can the great diversity which existed between the various aboriginal tribes of America, at the time of its discovery, be satisfactorily accounted for.

These may be divided roughly into the long-headed and the short-headed people, though many transitional forms are found. They correspond to the long-headed northern, and the short-headed southern mongoloid types of Asia.

The long heads were probably the first to arrive, but were driven southward by the short heads, of whom the Maya were perhaps the most typical representatives.

Excavations in the Valley of Mexico, in recent years, have brought to light evidence of the existence of at least three main civilizations, which successively followed each other there in the past. These may be divided into an almost infinite number of subgroups.

The uppermost stratigraphic layer of the soil represents the Aztec occupation, the most recent of these contemporary, in the valley, with the coming of the Spaniards.

This layer contains immense quantities of domestic utensils, incense burners, and images in pottery, with spindle whorls, beads, axe, spear, and arrow heads, and other typically Aztec artifacts in bone, stone, copper, and clay.

Beneath this, to a depth of from six to ten feet, is found a layer containing relics of the Toltec occupation. This people belonged to the same Nahua stock as the Aztecs, but arrived in the valley some seven or eight centuries before the latter.

They reached a high state of civilization, and built the great pyramids of the sun and moon at Teotihuacan, where vast numbers of beautifully modelled little pottery figurines, perhaps the most typical product of their culture, are found.

There was evidently considerable communication between them and the Maya of Yucatan, for numbers of Maya artifacts have been found in the Toltec area, and many of the Maya gods were adopted by the Toltecs, together with the calendar and other distinctive products of Maya civilization.

The lowest stratigraphic layer varies from ten to

twenty feet in thickness, and represents the accumulations of a much longer period of time than the other two combined.

It contains the relics of the earliest civilization developed in the Valley of Mexico, and indeed, so far as we know at present, of the earliest civilization, recognizable as such, evolved upon the American continent. This culture, usually known as the "Archaic," was probably the most widely spread of all the civilizations of the Western Hemisphere, for traces of it are to be found from the Mexican plateau to the highlands of Colombia and Ecuador.

The relics left by these Archaic people are highly characteristic, and easily to be recognized whenever found.

Human figurines, modelled in clay, are of very frequent occurrence, and, though somewhat grotesque, are not without a certain virility and strength in their modelling.

The eyes and mouth protrude from the face, and are usually indicated by oval or circular appliqué bands of clay. The limbs are crudely moulded, and the fingers and toes indicated by a series of incised lines at their extremities. The domestic pottery is rough and crude; three-legged pots, with a face moulded at the extremity of each hollow leg, are of frequent occurrence. Small statuettes in stone are sometimes found, and both stone and pottery figurines frequently represent individuals going about their ordinary occupations, a woman nursing her child or holding a pot, a man beating a drum or carrying a burden on his back, and the like. They resemble, in fact, very closely, both in their crudeness and realism, the small cinerary figures found at Santa Rita, which belong to the late Maya-Toltec period.

It is difficult, on stratigraphic evidence alone, to date this Archaic material with any degree of accuracy, as a considerable proportion of the medium in which it is embedded consists of volcanic ash and mud, the rate and period of the formation of which it is impossible to estimate. We are, however, fortunately provided with another and more accurate guide.

At Coyoacan, and other places in the Valley of Mexico, there occurred an extensive inundation of molten lava, covering the surface of the soil to a depth of from ten to fifteen feet. On geological evidence this flow cannot have taken place more recently than toward the end of the second millennium B.C.

Beneath this lava flow, extensive traces of the Archaic civilization have been brought to light, including graves, houses, and innumerable artifacts, indicating a very respectable antiquity for this comparatively high aboriginal American culture, even when compared with those of the Old World.

In Guatemala, Spanish and British Honduras, and other points throughout the Maya area, there have recently been brought to light extensive remains of this Archaic culture, one of the most characteristic of which is, perhaps, a stone, shaped somewhat like a celt, upon which is roughly outlined, in sunk lines, a crude human figure.

The occurrence of these Archaic objects throughout the Maya area would seem to indicate either that the country was at one time occupied by the Archaic people, or that the Maya were themselves descendants of the Archaics, and retained, possibly for ceremonial reasons, a number of these curious figurines manufactured by their remote ancestors. Again, it is possible that the technique of manufacture of these objects may have been handed down continuously amongst the Maya from their Archaic ancestors.

In the state of Vera Cruz, Mexico, are found two Indian tribes, the Totonac and the Huaxtec, whose territory extends as far north as the Panuco River.

Both of these speak a dialect of Maya, and possess strong cultural affinities with the southern Maya, yet excavation in the Valley of the Panuco has shown that its early archæology is almost exactly identical with that of the Archaic found in the Mexican Valley. We encounter, in fact, the curious condition of a Maya linguistic islet in the midst of a sea of totally unallied languages, separated from the Chontal, its nearest linguistic affinity, by nearly 500 miles.

To the south of these tribes, at San Andres Tuxtla, also in the State of Vera Cruz, has been found the earliest, deciphered, Maya date, inscribed upon a small greenstone figurine, known as the Tuxtla Statuette, recording a day in Katun 6 of Baktun 8 in Maya chronology, which, according to Spinden's correlation, corresponds to the year 100 B.C.

Spinden's correlation between Maya and Christian chronology has been adopted throughout this book, not because its accuracy is beyond doubt, but because it affords a convenient method of fitting the known Maya dates into their relative places in Christian chronology. If the Goodman correlation be accepted, the count will have to be shifted forward 260 years, and if the correlation usually accepted in Germany be accepted, it must be shifted back a similar period.

Up to the present, the earliest date found inscribed upon a stela is at Uaxactun, in the Peten province of Guatemala, recording Katun 14 of Bactun 8, in Maya chronology, corresponding to the year 68 A.D.

It would appear then that this Archaic people, highlanders and agriculturalists, flourished between the first and third millennia B.C. upon the mountain plateaux between Mexico and Colombia, where they developed a very characteristic civilization of their own.

They were, no doubt, the direct descendants of one of the nomadic tribes from Asia, the first American explorers, who had crossed the Behring Straits perhaps 10,000 years before.

They must have been, however, agriculturalists of no mean order, for to them we owe the cultivation of the maize plant, that staple food of all tropical and subtropical America. It seems probable that maize was developed originally by intensive cultivation from the teosinte (*Euchlæna mexicana*), found throughout the plateau country of Mexico and Guatemala, as this is the only known plant with which maize can be crossed. The gap between teosinte and cultivated maize is, it must be admitted, an exceedingly wide one, and it must have taken many centuries to evolve the one from the other.

The existence of these tillers of the stony and barren hill and plateau soils must have been a hard one, how hard, one has only to live amongst the modern agricultural hill tribes of Guatemala and Spanish Honduras to realize, for these dwell under very similar conditions to their Archaic ancestors, with whom they are almost exactly on a par culturally. Bound to the soil by the constant and unremitting attention demanded by the poor land, life must have been a constant and never-ending fight with starvation, leaving little leisure for art, architecture, or exploration of the country remote from their own immediate settlements.

Nevertheless, at some time in the first millennium B.C., a band of this Archaic people, either more adventurous than their neighbors, or, more probably, driven thereto by shortness of food, did migrate toward the coast, which they reached, probably somewhere in the neighborhood of the Panuco River Valley.

Once having arrived at the fertile lowlands near the coast, there can be no doubt that the Archaic civilization rapidly underwent an extraordinary efflorescence, and made more progress in centuries, under the stimulating and favorable conditions of a warm climate, a fertile soil, and a plentiful and easily procured food supply, with ample leisure for the cultivation of science, and the fine arts, which these connoted, than it had in millennia under the harsh and withering conditions of the hill country from which it had come.

How long the wanderers remained in the neighborhood of their first settlement, in the vicinity of the Panuco Valley, we have no means of knowing, but the probability is that they left before much progress had been made in the development of ceramics, sculpture, architecture, and the calendar system which characterized their later civilization. Had these been developed, the Huaxtecas, who were evidently a section of the people left behind in their old home when the migration commenced, must inevitably have retained some traces of them. But they have not done so, and have in fact developed an entirely different culture of their own. Consequently, it is fairly certain that the split took place when the affinities between the two people were purely and solely linguistic.

It was, probably, toward the end of the first millennium B.C. that the Maya set out on the migration southward and eastward, which led them toward the Peten district of Guatemala, where, toward the end of the first century A.D., they founded Uaxactun, the earliest of those great cities, the ruins of which, fifteen centuries later, were to astonish the first European explorers in the New World.

If the record of the Tuxtla Statuette is to be relied on, the Maya must have passed the neighborhood of Vera Cruz, which is about half way between the Panuco Valley and Uaxactun, toward the end of the second century B.C., and at that time their calendar system, at least, had apparently been completely developed.

Doctor Morley believes that the Maya were originally a nomadic tribe, living in the Gulf Coast plain of Mexico, between Tuxpam and the Panuco River, unacquainted with agriculture, and living in a state of continuous struggle for bare existence, occupying temporary shelters, and constantly moving from place to place in search of food.

Amongst these nomads there arrived immigrants from the Archaic people of the highlands of Mexico, bringing with them their knowledge of agriculture, and more particularly of the cultivation of corn, rapidly changing the people from nomadic hunters to settled agriculturalists, with leisure, which they had never before enjoyed owing to the exigencies of their search after food, for the development of art, science, and religion.

Our knowledge of the rise and fall of the ancient Maya civilization is derived from five main sources.

A. Contemporaneous records from the time of the Conquest, by Spanish and native writers, the most important of whom are Landa, Cogolludo, and Villagutierre.

These all described the Maya as they found them, in

Courtesy of the Field Museum

PLATE I. THE MAYA AREA WITH PRINCIPAL CITIES

Yucatan, at the time of the Conquest, but it must be borne in mind that the Maya civilization which had reached its apogee nearly 1,000 years before, had been undergoing a gradual process of degeneration since that period, so that material differences probably existed between the religion and social customs of the Maya of the Old Empire, and those of Yucatan at the coming of the Spaniards.

Landa, Bishop of Yucatan soon after the Conquest, deals with the religion, chronology, social life, and laws of the Maya, of which he probably knew more than any other European of his day. To his bigotry, unfortunately, we owe the irreparable loss of the great mass of aboriginal Maya literature, burned in Merida by his order.

Father Diego Cogolludo, in his history of Yucatan from the Conquest to the Independence, gives a graphic picture of the manners and customs of the people, their laws and arithmetical and chronological systems, though he wastes a good deal of space in chronicling minor ecclesiastical events and squabbles.

Villagutierre, in his *Conquista de Itza*, published in 1701, only a few years after its occurrence, gives a graphic account of the Conquest by the Spaniards of the Indians of Peten, the last stronghold of the Maya to hold out against them. He describes the manners and customs, dress, religion, social life, and laws of this last independent remnant of the Maya.

B. The Codices. These are native books produced by

the Maya themselves, before the Conquest. They were made from the fibre of the *Agave americana,* from which it is possible to construct a very tough, durable paper. This was covered with a white size, upon which the hieroglyphics were painted in various colors.

The early Spanish chroniclers tell us that these codices dealt with history, medicine, magic, divination, and astronomy. Unfortunately, the vast majority of them were, as before mentioned, burned by Bishop Landa at a great Auto de Fe, as, being creations of the devil, they tended to prevent the conversion of the natives to Christianity, and to encourage them in the continuance of their former idolatrous practices. Only three of these precious works have come down to us, all of them dealing with astronomical and calendaric matters, and the names of the gods who presided over various divisions of the 260-day period.

The first is known as the Dresden Codex, and is preserved in the public library at Dresden. It is by far the finest of the three, and belongs to the best period of the Maya New Empire, probably about 1000 A.D.

The Codex Peresianus is preserved in the Biblioteque Nationale in Paris, and is much inferior in execution to the Dresden Codex. It is executed in a style precisely similar to the wall paintings at the very late town of Tuluum, on the east coast of Yucatan, was probably produced in that town, possibly by one of the artists who executed the mural paintings on the temples there, and dates consequently from a period not very long before the Conquest.

The last codex, known as the Troano-Cortesian, is divided into two parts, each of which is in a different museum in Spain, though they are parts of the same codex. It is very poorly executed, by some one without any great technical skill in writing the hieroglyphics, and probably dates from after the Conquest.

It is a great misfortune that not a single historical codex has survived the bigotry of the early Spanish priests, but there still remains a possibility that one may turn up either in some private collection or library in Spain, northern Italy, or the Maya area, or even in the course of intensive excavation in some of the larger Maya cities, as Tikal, Palenque, or Copan, where but a very small amount of work of this kind has as yet been accomplished.

The recent discovery in a cave, by Mr. Blom of the Tulane University, of Maya cotton fabric, fifteen centuries old and still in an excellent state of preservation, encourages one to hope that at least some of the codices we know the Maya buried with their priests may have been similarly preserved.

C. Native historical records, written by the Maya before the Conquest, and later translated from their hieroglyphics into Spanish, by scholars who were acquainted with both languages.

The two most important of these records are known as the Books of Chilam-Balaam, and the Popul-Vuh.

The Books of Chilam-Balaam supply an exceedingly abridged and tenuous outline of Maya history from a certain Katun 8 Ahau, when the Maya are said to have left their original home in Tulapan, to another Katun 3 Ahau, when Father Fuensalida is reported to have first visited Lake Peten Itza.

The Katun is a twenty-year (or rather 7,200 day) period, and between the first and last date, 73 Katuns elapsed, covering a period of approximately 1,460 years.

Not every Katun, however, has events recorded against it, and, especially in the earlier parts of the chronicle, very wide lacunæ occur.

The first Katun 8 Ahau corresponds, according to Spinden's correlation, to the year 176 A.D., and between that and the next event recorded, namely, the arrival of the Maya at Chacnouitan, 4 Katuns, or nearly 80 years later, not a single event is recorded. The next lacuna is even greater, for, from their arrival in Chacnouitan to the discovery of Chichen-Itza, in Yucatan, 10 Katuns, or 197 years later, in 452 A.D., the record is silent. In the following Katun 4 Ahau, or 472 A.D., Bakhalal was occupied. In Katun 11 Ahau, or 531 A.D., Chichen-Itza was occupied. From 531 to 669, in which year Chichen-Itza was abandoned, no event is recorded.

In Katun 6 Ahau, or 709 A.D., Chakanputun was occupied, and at this place the Maya remained until Katun 8 Ahau, or 945 A.D., when, for some unknown reason, they abandoned it.

If the nation which has no history is a happy one, the Maya must have been one of the most fortunate nations on earth, for during the whole of their stay in Chakanputun, occupying 12 Katuns, or 236 years, not a single event occurred which was considered worth recording.

In Katun 6 Ahau, 965 A.D., the Itza returned to their old city of Chichen-Itza, which they had abandoned nearly 300 years before, and in Katun 2 Ahau, 1004 A.D., the Xiu founded in Yucatan the great city of Uxmal. In the same year was formed the League of Mayapan, between the Xiu of Uxmal, the Itza of Chichen-Itza, and the Cocomes of Mayapan, the three principal ruling clans of the Maya in the peninsula.

This confederation lasted for nearly two centuries, till Katun 8 Ahau, 1201 A.D.: when, owing to a quarrel having broken out between the Itzas and the Cocomes, it came to an end, the whole peninsula was plunged into internecine war. From 1004 to 1201 A.D., during the continuance of the League, the country experienced an artistic and scientific renaissance, after the dark ages which had passed since the Maya left their old cities in the south, about the middle of the sixth century A.D. After the breakup of the League, the country steadily degenerated, up to the arrival of the Spaniards, who found it divided into a multiplicity of small states constantly at war with each other, a condition which, as in the case of the conquest of the Aztecs by Cortez, materially assisted them in their subjugation of the natives.

The Popul-Vuh, or "Collection of Writings," is the sacred book of the Quichè and Kakchiquel Indians,

Plate II. ALTAR FROM THE ANCIENT CITY OF COPAN

branches of the great Maya family, probably descendants of those who had been left behind in the trek northward into Yucatan, on the break-up of the Old Empire, to be described later. This work is divided into four books. The greater part of the first three deal with legends and purely mythological events, but the fourth purports to give a history of the tribes from the earliest times, a good deal of which is probably somewhat apocryphal.

D. The Monuments, or Stelæ. The Maya were in the habit, during at least fifteen centuries, of erecting every twenty years, and in the larger cities every ten or five years, stone monoliths, recording the exact date upon which the stela was erected. In addition to this, the stela frequently had sculptured upon it a life-size human figure, in relief, possibly the contemporary high priest or king, together with a varying number of, at present, undeciphered hieroglyphics. These probably record briefly the principal events which had occurred during the period commemorated by the stela. The dates on these stones, however, are of most importance, and in order to comprehend them it is necessary to possess some knowledge of the Maya chronological system.

The Maya used the day as the unit, and they recorded only past time, as we do, when reading the time on a clock, though not when speaking of days, months, and years, when we illogically use current time.

Maya chronology started from a certain day 4 Ahau 8 Cumhu, beginning of a Baktun 13, falling in the year 3373 B.C. According to Spinden's correlation.

Any event in their history is fixed by recording the number of Baktuns, or 400-year periods, Katuns, or 20-year periods, Tuns, or years of 360 days, Uinals, or months of 20 days, and Kins, or days, which had elapsed since the commencing day 4 Ahau 8 Cumhu.

This system is known as the "Long Count." In addition to this, however, they employed the "Calendar Round," consisting of 18,980 named days, following each other in endless succession, one Calendar Round succeeding another through all time. On the stelæ are recorded, first, the exact number of days which had elapsed from the starting day of Maya chronology to the day upon which the stela was erected, and, as a check, the name of this day in the Calendar Round.

In addition to these, moreover, there is recorded a lunar time count, probably more for ceremonial reasons than with any idea of fixing the already doubly recorded date with any greater accuracy.

On many of the stelæ several dates are recorded, the last of which is almost invariably the contemporaneous date. On most of them are sculptured a large number of hieroglyphics which, so far as we know, have no calendaric significance, and it is only reasonable to suppose that these record the principal events which occurred during the period commemorated. Like the books of Chilam-Balaam, they probably give the meagrest possible outline of Maya history, by recording the occurrence of floods, famines, earthquakes, dynastic changes, and other outstanding events.

Considerable doubt exists as to whether the elaborately clothed and ornamented figures which usually occupy one surface of each of the stelæ are meant to represent gods, or merely portray high priests, kings, or other prominent contemporaneous individuals. I am inclined to accept the latter hypothesis, as the individuals portrayed, while conforming very closely to the common Maya facial type, and never exhibiting grotesque or animal heads such as are so frequently associated with the gods, yet possess a certain character and individuality which mark them out as portraits of living men.

The earliest date recorded on a stela is 8.14.0.0.0., or 8 Baktuns 14 Katuns, 0 Tuns, Uinals, and Kins, after the commencing day of Maya chronology, falling in the year 57 A.D. The elaborate chronological system was undoubtedly as highly developed at this early period as it was 1,500 years later, and as it must have required centuries for its complete elaboration, it is obvious that the dates must have been recorded previous to the first stela on some more perishable material than stone, probably Agave Americana paper, or, in the case of the stelæ, wood. Support is lent to this theory by the fact that the sculpture on the early monoliths is in low relief, and follows very closely the technique of wood carving, whereas in the later stelæ the figures stand out so far from the background as almost to approximate sculpture in the round.

At many of the Maya cities, large plane stelæ with

no sculpture upon them are found, and these were probably covered originally with skins of smooth stucco, upon which the hieroglyphics were painted; indeed, at least one stela still exists, around the base of which, where they had been protected from the weather by the accumulation of vegetal mould, these superimposed layers of painted stucco still adhere, indicating not only that the plane stelæ were originally covered with stucco, but that this was, like the stucco decorating the interior walls of the temples, renewed from time to time.

E. Oral traditions. When the Spaniards first arrived in Yucatan, they found the natives under the complete domination of a priesthood, who carried out a complex and elaborate ritual connected with the worship of a great number of gods and goddesses. In addition to this, the priests were the magicians and soothsayers, and they alone understood the complicated calendar hierogly-phics, which enabled them to designate lucky and un-lucky days for fishing, hunting, agricultural operations, marrying, setting out on a journey, and in fact for every conceivable human activity. Furthermore they were the sole possessors of any knowledge of medicine, astronomy, and mathematics, and it was they who fixed the days and divisions of the 260-day ritual year, upon which the festivals of the gods who presided over each had to be celebrated.

The lower classes, like the proletariat of all times and all countries, seem to have possessed but a scant and superficial knowledge of their complex religion, confined chiefly to a familiarity with the prayers appropriate for certain important occasions, particularly those connected with felling the bush for plantations, sowing and reaping the maize, and other agricultural operations. They were also expert in the manufacture of ceremonial incense burners of clay, with crude images of the gods portrayed on their exteriors, which were used in most of the religious ceremonies in which the common people participated. In addition to this every craft and trade had its own gods, as, those of the gold workers, stone workers, fishermen, weavers, etc., to whom they built little shrines, where offerings of food, flowers, beads, clay images, and other objects were made.

On the arrival of the Spaniards and the complete subjugation of the country, the unfortunate Indians found themselves between the upper millstone of the Conquistadors and the nether millstone of the priests. The former had but one object in view, the enrichment of themselves, by the acquisition of such treasure in precious metals, or stones, and other valuables as the natives might possess, and when this source of revenue was exhausted, in their complete enslavement, and in wringing from them, by means of forced labor, on the land, the ultimate farthing they were able to produce.

The ecclesiastics, moved by a fanaticism almost inconceivable to us at the present day, at once set about the salvation of the heathens' souls, and not infrequently proved even more cruel in the attainment of their object than the Conquistadors themselves.

Their ancient books were burned, their idols destroyed, their religious ceremonies forbidden under the cruelest penalties, and their priests driven into the remotest fastnesses of the bush to practise the rites and ceremonies of their ancient religion. This persecution rapidly resulted in a complete loss of the knowledge possessed by the priests of the ancient written language, religious ceremonies, astronomy, medicine, and history, which had been handed down for more than 1,500 years from the Maya of the Old Empire, and added to century by century by the Maya of Yucatan. There were still left, however, members of the minor priesthood, Mens, and Chaacs, who were capable of repeating by rote the prayers suitable for the varying seasons, to the rain god, the wind god, and other gods of fertility.

They were also expert at manufacturing images of the gods, and censors for burning copal at the various religious ceremonies, and of going through the long and complicated ritual enjoined each year on certain feasts connected with agriculture, in which the various offerings of food and drink to be made to the gods were prescribed with meticulous exactness.

It is practically certain that, in a very few years after the Conquest, knowledge of the hieroglyphics and the calendar system, involving the Long Count, and the Calendar Round, already described, had become obsolete.

How much of the other religious and calendaric knowledge survived, it is impossible to say, for naturally the Indians, who were nearly all compulsorily baptized, soon began to realize the terrible penalties which were immediately visited in this world on those perverts who reverted to their former idolatrous practices, with a promise of certain and eternal damnation in the next. In consequence of this persecution, all those who wished to practise the rites of their ancient religion and perhaps to petition their ancient gods for deliverance from the hard yoke of the Spaniards, and a return to the old, easy, joyous, carefree life, retired into the innermost fastnesses of the bush to do so at a safe distance from the ever-prying eyes of some zealous monk or lay brother. When interrogated by anyone with possible Spanish leanings, they would naturally disclaim any knowledge of, or participation in, the ancient religion. For these reasons, it was believed, till comparatively recently, that the old faith had completely died out, and that no traditions of it survived amongst even the last descendants of the Maya in Yucatan.

But we live in more enlightened times, and the Indian, no longer fearing religious persecution, has in some places reverted to the open practice of the old religion, showing that somehow, and somewhere, the spark, though carefully concealed, must have been kept alive through nearly four centuries of persecution, only awaiting a favorable opportunity to be again kindled into fire.

As one would naturally expect, the ancient ceremonies and ritual have survived best in those two remote portions of the Maya area where the Spaniards never succeeded in completely subjugating the natives. The Lacondones, living along the banks of the Rio de la Pasion, in southern Mexico, still dress and live as their forefathers dressed and lived before the Conquest. Unfortunately, as far as can be ascertained, no knowledge of the hieroglyphics or the calendar survives amongst them, but they worship the old gods, in whose honor they carry out the appropriate ceremonies at the various seasons. They even manufacture crude censors of clay, with the heads of the gods outside, which they carry to the temples built by their ancestors nearly 2,000 years ago, now mere heaps of ruins buried in the virgin bush, where they burn incense in them to the images of the old gods, and then leave them as offerings on the spot.

Amongst the Santa Cruz Indians, along the east coast of Yucatan, who have never been entirely subdued, and amongst the Maya Indians of British Honduras, the old ceremonies are freely practised, and definite orders of minor priests still exist amongst them, who pass down their knowledge of the ancient rites, generation after generation, to suitable aspirants to the priesthood. Amongst the hill Indians of Guatemala, also, the old religion has a strong hold, for they enjoyed a long immunity from Spanish persecution, owing to their extreme poverty, and the unproductive soil and sparse population of their country.

CHAPTER II

HISTORY OF THE OLD EMPIRE
(T. G.)

Maya of the Old Empire lived exclusively in the stone age. Earliest stela at Uaxactun and its significance. Description of the city, the first founded by the Maya. Astronomical observatory. Human sacrifice. The city of Tikal. Wood carving. Tzibanchè and its peculiar temples. The city of Copan. Beautiful stelæ. An astronomical congress in 503 A.D. Stylistic development of sculpture. An immense sun dial, four miles across. The city of Tuluum, founded 304 A.D., reoccupied 1,000 years later. Painted stucco walls. Pusilhà, a provincial site. Stratification. Lubaantum and its figurines. The only Maya stone bridge still in existence. Ichpaatun. Piedras Negras and its perfect series of hotun markers. Altar de Sacrificios. Palenque, the artistic centre of the Maya world. Beautiful mouldings in stucco. The Maya's accurate conception of the age of the universe. Yaxha. Yaxchilan. Accurate picture of the Old-Empire costumes afforded by the sculptures here. Tzendales. Itsimte. Nakum. Xultun. Quirigua, its beautiful stelæ and zoomorphic altars. Cobà and the great causeway. Seibal. A number of small, briefly occupied cities founded toward the end of the Old Empire. The Maya area and its mode of colonization. Stylistic classification of the sculptures. Well-marked periods. Political relations between the Maya Old-Empire cities. The exodus from the southern cities into Yucatan. Various reasons ascribed for this. None of them entirely satisfactory.

THE Maya, in their march of nearly 400 miles from the neighborhood of San Andres Tuxtla in the State of Vera Cruz to Uaxactun in the Peten district of Guatemala, must have occupied a period of approximately 168 years, for, as we have seen, the only dated relic left by them at San Andres records the year 100 B.C., while the first dated stela at Uaxactun records the Maya date

8.14.10.13.15., 8 Men 8 Kayab, or, June 16th, 68 A.D. This long period of wandering through forest and swamp was, no doubt, occupied mainly in seeking a suitable site in which to form a permanent settlement, but as they left behind them nowhere any trace of their passage, in the form of architectural remains, stelæ, or other characteristic objects, it would appear that, till their arrival in Uaxactun, no suitable site had presented itself.

Even admitting that no great number of people took part in this exodus from their northern home, it would probably have been necessary for them to make long halts, of perhaps a year or two, at very frequent intervals, in order to grow the corn necessary for food on the march. For this purpose the virgin bush had first to be felled, and allowed to dry in the sun, and then to be burned; finally, corn had to be planted over the burned area, and allowed to ripen. These various agricultural operations would, of necessity, have occupied a long time, as the Maya were living entirely in the stone age, and felling a tract of forest sufficiently large to produce corn for any considerable number of people, with no other tools than stone axes, must have been a long and arduous undertaking, necessitating a stay of at least two years at every halting place.

The vast majority of the Maya stelæ were erected to commemorate the passage of five, ten, or twenty-year periods, but the first stela at Uaxactun is an exception, as it bears an irregular date, that is, one containing an odd number of days and months, and was obviously erected to commemorate some extremely important event which occurred upon that date. The stela is a large one, standing nine feet two inches above ground and its quarrying, removal to the site selected for it, and the sculpture upon it of hieroglyphic inscription, all performed solely with the aid of stone tools, must have occupied a considerable time, and were probably not completed till many years after the date which it commemorates. Beside the stela stands a flat, roughly circular altar. This is obviously an older stela, cut down to form an altar, for on both sides of it are sculptured human figures which have been partly broken away to give the stone its conventional round shape.

Now, the Maya frequently broke up and re-used the sculptured stones of their ancestors, either because the events they recorded had faded from men's minds, and were no longer considered worthy of commemoration, or possibly, because the art of the sculptor appeared crude and archaic to the new generation. We are, therefore, led to the conclusion that the stela which was trimmed down to form an altar in front of our 68 A.D. stela was considerably older than the latter, and that it either was considered an eyesore from an artistic point of view, or recorded events so remote from 68 A.D., as to be no longer of interest to men then living.

The physical conditions of the surrounding country at Uaxactun were probably somewhat different, when the Maya first reached the site, to those prevailing at the present day. Now, the sole water supply is derived from a small water hole, which, though in the rainy season it expands into a good sized lagoon, in the dry season contains no water at all. Either this water hole has become largely silted up, or the Maya were able to store water in those curious subterraneous chambers, hollowed out in the limestone, great numbers of which are found in the vicinity of nearly all the large ruined sites.

What may be termed the Capitol, at Uaxactun, was built on the summit of a small hill, apparently artificially flattened for the purpose. It contained the temples, plazas, open courts, and commemorative stelæ, with the private residences of the rulers and chief priests connected with the temple worship. The whole is now in a more or less ruinous condition, and not one building remains intact. From the top of this Capitol a magnificient view is obtained of the surrounding country, which in the days of the city's greatness was doubtless covered with the thatched wooden houses of the poorer people, beyond which extended in all directions a green ring of growing maize, the main support of the people.

To the east of the Capitol is a second group of buildings, consisting of temples standing on pyramidal substructures, stelæ, and altars, grouped around a large central court. To the west of the court is a lofty, steep, stone-faced pyramid, fifty feet high, in front of which stands a stela, upon which is recorded the end of Katun

Plate III. MONOLITH FROM THE ANCIENT CITY OF COPAN

3 of Baktun 9, or 235 A.D. On the opposite side of the central court is a large, stone-faced, truncated pyramid, upon the summit of which stand three temples in a row.

It was found that lines of sight between this stela and the temples were respectively twenty-four degrees north and south of east. In other words, the whole complex of plaza, temples and stela is nothing more nor less than an astronomical observatory, recording the positions at which the sun rose at the spring and autumn equinoxes, and at the summer and winter solstices.

Each of the three temples contained a rectangular, hollow, stone altar, in which were found a number of beautiful objects of jade and pottery, no doubt placed there as offerings to the gods to whom the temples were dedicated. With these were several human heads, severed, in the upper cervical region, from the bodies to which they belonged, and it would appear that the Maya, even at this early date, cannot be absolved from the crime of human sacrifice, which it was formerly believed was not introduced amongst them till some eleven centuries later, by Nahua immigrants from the Valley of Mexico.

The latest date recorded at the city is 10.3.0.0.0., or 639 A.D., consequently it was occupied for a period of at least 571 years, and probably for much longer, since, as we have seen, there is reason for supposing that there existed at least one stela more ancient than that recording 68 A.D., while it is hardly probable that the whole of the inhabitants deserted the city, en masse, after the erection of the last stela. The city was not only the first, and one of the last of all the Maya cities to be occupied, but it was occupied over a longer consecutive period than any of the others.

The Maya remained for approximately 120 years in Uaxactun, no doubt building the temples and palaces whose ruins now remain. At the end of this period, they sent out a colony to a site some fifteen miles to the southwest, where they founded the great city of Tikal, afterwards to become the largest, and perhaps the most important of all the Maya cities. The earliest date recorded here is 9.0.10.0.0., or 185 A.D., and the last 10.2.0.0.0., 609 A.D., so that the city was occupied continuously for a period of 424 years. The buildings are finer, more imposing, and owing to the great thickness of their walls, in a better state of preservation than those found at any of the other Old Empire sites. The unit in laying out the city was the quadrangular plaza, round which were clustered the temple and dwellings of the priests. These were added to, century by century, till the city reached gigantic proportions, connoting a very large population, probably a quarter of a million or more.

There are three great acropolises, natural hills terraced, faced with stone, and having their summits truncated for the reception of stone buildings. Five main temples exist, all of which stand upon lofty, almost perpendicular stone-faced pyramids. They are approached by steep flights of stone steps, and are surmounted by high roof combs. The loftiest of these is 230 feet in height. All the buildings at Tikal, whether temples or residences, stand upon stone-faced substructures, and are approached by flights of stone steps. Some of the residential buildings contain as many as twenty rooms. The art of wood carving was developed, at Tikal, to an extent unknown at any of the other Maya cities, and some of the lintels and beams of sapote wood, upon which are depicted gods, men, and grotesque figures, might compare favorably with the work of the best modern wood carver. The last date recorded at the city was 609 A.D., but it is certain that it was occupied long after this period, as graffiti, scratched upon the smooth stucco of the interior walls of many of the temples, are very common, and it is obvious that these would only have been placed there after the temples had ceased to serve their original purpose.

To the west of the Bacalar lagoon in Quintana Roo, Mexico, is found the ruined city of Tzibanche, where the only date recorded is inscribed upon a wooden lintel, and has not at present been definitely deciphered. This town possesses a number of very lofty temples, standing upon steep substructures, approached by flights of steps. The height of the building is increased by the addition of lofty hollow roof combs. From the style of its architecture, and the presence of wood carving, this city was obviously inspired by Tikal, and belongs to the same period.

The next great city founded by the Maya was Copan,

in the Republic of Spanish Honduras, nearly 300 miles due south of Uaxactun. The first date recorded here is 9.1.0.0.0., or 195 A.D., and the last is 9.18.10.0.0., or 540 A.D., so that the city was occupied for a period of at least 345 years.

The main group, or acropolis, at Copan is an immense, complicated mass of courts, plazas, temples, pyramids, and stairways, which during the three and a half centuries occupancy of the city were added to, enlarged, and built over, till the original structures can only be observed in an archæological section, cut by the river to a depth of 114 feet beneath the level of the present top of the structure.

Around the acropolis are innumerable minor groups of ruins, extending over almost the whole of the floor of the Copan Valley.

Situated upon two hill tops, one almost due east, the other almost due west of the city, are two stone monuments, now fallen and broken. Both recorded Maya dates. That upon one reads 9.10.19.13.0., 3 Ahau 8 Yaxkin, or, September 6th, 392 A.D., that upon the other includes this date between two others recorded upon it. Doctor Spinden believes that these two stelæ formed a gigantic sundial, no less than four and a half miles across, and that the sun, as viewed from the eastern stela, set behind the western, every year, upon a date which the Maya regarded as the beginning of their agricultural year. This corresponded to April 5 of our year, but was afterward shifted to April 9, when the

Plate IV. ASTRONOMICAL CONFERENCE AT COPAN IN THE SIXTH CENTURY, PROBABLY
THE FIRST IN THE WORLD

sun set directly in a line with the stelæ twice in each year, on April 9th and September 2nd.

On one of the altars at Copan is a sculpture in low relief, which appears to portray a congress of Astronomer-priests, which took place in the city on September 2, 503 A.D., and which may have been connected with the changing of the date from September 9th to September 2nd.

Copan possesses a magnificent array of large sculptured stelæ, showing the stylistic development which took place, from the earliest to the latest years of the city's history. The relief of the sculpture was at first very low, but developed, Katun by Katun, till the figures stood out from the background, almost in the round, while the pose of the human figure, at first stiff and formal, later showed considerable knowledge of perspective, and in its presentation in profile was almost perfect, and certainly superior to any of the results obtained along these lines in either Egypt or Mesopotamia.

Near the town of Ococingo, close to the Mexico-Guatemala boundary, are found the ruins of Tonina. The earliest date recorded here is 9.6.0.0.0., the latest, 9.19.0.0.0. The city was consequently occupied for a period of at least 13 Katuns, or 260 years.

The next city founded by the Maya, if the evidence of the dated stela is to be accepted, was Tuluum, on the east coast of Yucatan, nearly 400 miles north of Uaxactun. Only a single stela has been found there, recording the date 9.6.10.0.0., or 304 A.D. Why the Maya should have made this long march northward, through swamps and forest, to settle by the coast, on infertile lands, both of which conditions they carefully avoided elsewhere, it is impossible to say. Their stay at Tuluum was not a long one, as but one stela was erected there, though the site was occupied 1,000 years later by Maya of the New Empire, who built a town of considerable size and importance on the ancient site, which was occupied right up to the coming of the Spaniards. It may be that Tuluum was occupied continuously from 304 A.D. up to the sixteenth century, as the last inhabitants evidently revered the stela of the early settlers, which they even housed in a special temple of its own, and it is quite conceivable that after the exodus of the first founders, a few inhabitants remained behind, though not sufficient to undertake the periodical erection of stelæ, and that their descendants were sufficiently reinforced by fugitives after the fall of Mayapan to found the new city of Tuluum, which the first Spanish explorers describe as being "as fine as Sevilla."

Tuluum is one of the few Maya towns surrounded by a great stone wall, evidently built for defensive purposes, as it is provided with sally ports, and guarded at intervals by watch towers. Such a wall would render it possible for a small force to hold the city against a vastly greater number of assailants, armed only with bow and arrows and spears.

The next city founded was Pusilhà, on the river of

that name, in British Honduras, situated about midway between Uaxactun and Copan. The earlier stela at this site records the date 9.7.0.0.0., or 314 A.D., the latest, 9.15.0.0.0., or 371 A.D. This was obviously a provincial site, as, though there are a number of both stelæ and altars, the workmanship is poor, and the technique crude.

A cave was found here, which had evidently been used as a rubbish depository, or kitchen midden, throughout the entire history of the city. It provided a stratigraphic record of the pottery and implements used from the earliest to the latest times, which seems to indicate that this town was the principal source from whence came that beautiful, porcelain-like, painted ware, which is found only very rarely at other sites. In Pusilhà the fragments of many hundreds of vessels of this ware were found, covered with hieroglyphics, and figures of gods, men, animals, and flowers, and geometrical devices, colored red, yellow, white, black, and green. Some of this pottery is also very tastefully decorated with incised devices, for the most part geometrical in design, in low relief. Pusilhà is unique amongst Maya towns in possessing the stone abutments of a bridge over the Pusilhà River, built by the ancient inhabitants, still in situ, and almost as perfect as they were when first erected about the fourth century A.D.

Close to Pusilhà are the ruins of Lubaantun, which probably belong to the same period, though no dated stela has been found as yet. The buildings here consist of immense pyramids, divided by courts and plazas, and faced with blocks of cut stone. They were probably used as substructures for wooden temples and houses, which have long since become incorporated with the surrounding humus.

Vast numbers of clay figurines were found at this site, of men, women, and children going about their ordinary avocations. All classes are represented, from the laborer with a load over his back, to the king borne along in his palanquin by gorgeously arrayed retainers. There was evidently close communication between Pusilhà and Lubaantun, in ancient times, for a good deal of the pottery manufactured at the former is found at Lubaantun, and quite a number of figurines from the latter appear at Pusilhà.

The next city founded by the Maya was at Ichpaatun, on the Chetumal Bay, in Quintana Roo. The only stela at this site records the date 9.8.0.0.0., or 333 A.D. The pyramidal substructures found here closely resemble those at Lubaantun, and both they and the stela probably belong to the same period. The site itself, however, is surrounded by a stone wall, doubtless for defensive purposes, and this part of the town is probably contemporaneous with Tuluum, where a similar wall exists, and with other sites on the east coast of Yucatan.

About this period was founded Cobà, in the north of Yucatan, to the east of Chichen-Itza, and between that city and the sea. The architecture here, while distinctively Old Empire in type, has many features which suggest New Empire influence, and also free communication with Tuluum and Lubaantun. A great raised stone road extends for miles from this city in the direction of Chichen-Itza, though it is difficult to assign any reason for the immense outlay in time and energy which the construction of this vast causeway must have necessitated, as the Maya used neither beasts of burden nor wheeled vehicles, and the road does not cross any swamp, which without it would have been impassable in wet weather. The only explanation appears to be that it was constructed as a via sacra, for the people of Cobà, which was a town of considerable importance, for ceremonial processions to the great sacred city of Chichen-Itza, and its Cenote of Sacrifice.

Fifteen years later than Ichpaatun, in 9.8.15.0.0., or 348 A.D., was established the city of Piedras Negras, on the Usumacintla River, near the boundary line between Mexico and Guatemala, and about 160 miles west of Uaxactun. The earliest date recorded at this city is 9.8.15.0.0., and the latest 9.18.5.0.0., or 535 A.D., so that the site was occupied for a period of at least 187 years.

There are found here an extraordinarily perfect series of stelæ and altars, recording hotun, or five-year period endings. There are exactly thirty-nine monuments and just thirty-nine hotun endings between the date upon the first and last monument, so that, although at present not all the dates have been deciphered, it is reasonable to suppose that the series was originally complete from the first to the last hotun ending recorded. Many fine buildings are found at Piedras Negras, standing upon pyramidal substructures, and it was evidently a city of considerable importance, and large population. About 9.10.0.0.0., or 373 A.D., there was founded, some 120 miles southwest of Uaxactun, the small city of Altar de Sacrificios, closely adjoining which is El Pabellon. Three dates are found at these, extending from 9.10.0.0.0. to 9.14.0.0.0., or 452 A.D., and judging by the number of stelæ now indecipherable, it is probable that one was erected here at the end of every ten-year period.

In the same Katun 10, we find the earliest recorded date at the great city of Palenque, which may be regarded as the artistic centre of the Old Empire cities. It is situated in the State of Chiapas, Mexico, approximately 220 miles west of Uaxactun, and was the extreme western outpost of the Maya area.

The buildings are grouped around an immense one-storied structure, known as the palace, standing upon the summit of a truncated hill. It is surrounded by an inner and outer gallery, and contains an intricate mass of chambers, corridors, and open courts. Perhaps its most interesting feature is a small, three-storied, square tower, the only one of its kind now in existence in the Maya area. It was, like the round tower at Chichen-Itza, built eight centuries later by the Maya of the Second Empire, probably used as an astronomical observatory.

There is but a single stela known at Palenque, bearing the date 9.10.10.0.0., or 373 A.D., indeed, the paucity of all dates at such a large and important city is remarkable. The latest of these, recorded on a wall plaque, is 9.13.0.0.0., or 432 A.D., but it is impossible that such a vast number of magnificent edifices could have been constructed within little more than half a century; moreover, on stylistic grounds, many of the monuments belong to Katun 18 of Bactun 9, or at least a century later. Palenque is perhaps most celebrated for its magnificent stucco mouldings, depicting gods, and men, in elaborate costumes and headdresses. The sculptured wall panels, representing religious scenes and offerings to the gods, are amongst the most beautiful and artistic in the Maya area.

There is recorded at Palenque, in a building known as the "Temple of Inscription," a date composed of seven periods, namely, 1 Kin, 12 Uinals, 1 Tun, 8 Katuns, 1 Bactun, 18 Pictuns (8,000-year periods), and 7 Cabaltuns (160,000-year periods). If these numbers be added they will be found to amount to 455,393,401 days, or nearly 1,247,653 years.

At only two other Maya sites are dates found recording numbers composed of more than the usual five periods; one of these is at Copan, where six periods are recorded, and the other is at Tikal, where 8 periods are recorded, involving the stupendous span of 1,841,639,-800 days, or approximately 5,000,000 years. The very fact that the Maya were able to conceive of such immense periods of time in connection with the earth indicates a much juster appreciation on their part of its possible age than was possessed, probably, by any nation up to the nineteenth century.

Spinden believes that the Maya recognized three important historical epochs. The earliest, commencing in 13.0.0.0.0., 4 Ahau, 8 Cumhu, or October 14, 3373 B.C., he calls the Mundane Epoch, recording probably the date of some mythological event. Next came the Historical Epoch, commencing on 7.0.0.0.0., or 613 B.C., and finally the Epoch of the Chronicles commencing on the first day of Bactun 9, or February 10, 176 A.D. If this be accepted, the dates recorded in more than five periods must have recorded some such events as the birth of the gods, or the creation of the universe.

The ruined city of Palenque and its suburbs have never been accurately surveyed, and the most divergent views as to its extent are held by different travellers, varying from nine square miles to one square mile. If the scattered pyramids and single buildings, found for miles around, are to be included in the city's limits, the first two estimates would probably be the more accurate.

In 9.11.5.0.0., 397 A.D., or some fifteen years after Palenque, the small city of Yaxha, situated on the lagoon of the same name, about thirty miles southeast of Uaxactun, was founded by the Maya. It was originally a city of some importance, about three kilometres long, though exceptionally narrow, but is now in a very ruinous condition. Six stelæ are found here, but only one date has been deciphered up to the present.

Yaxchilan, situated on the borders of Peten and Mexico, was founded at about this period. It occupies the side of a small mountain range, and, judging by the number and size of the buildings, must have been a site of considerable importance. Four separate groups of buildings are recognizable; one, consisting of twenty temples, occupies the northeast slope of the range, a series of eight temples occupies the foot of the range, six further structures are found higher up, and the range is crowned by one large and one smaller acropolis. Yaxchilan is celebrated for its beautifully carved stone lintels, exhibiting for the most part priests and votaries engaged in sacrificial and ceremonial acts. The costumes and headdresses, with their extraordinarily elaborate decorations, consisting of feathers, tassels, studs, and jewels, are shown with the utmost minuteness, and give one a wonderfully accurate picture of the ceremonial dress of the upper class, amongst the Maya of that period. Although there are twenty stelæ at Yaxchilan, most of the dates have not been deciphered, and it would appear that the custom, so common throughout the Maya area, of erecting stelæ every five years, was not adhered to here.

The little city of Tzendales, in the State of Chiapas, Mexico, and about 200 miles southwest of Uaxactun, was the next city founded by the Maya, and bears but a single date, 9.13.0.0.0., or 432 A.D.

Twenty years later, in Katun 14, of Bactun 9, the city of Itsimte was founded. It is situated in the Peten district, some eighty miles southwest of Uaxactun. Four dated monuments are found here, all recording ten-year periods, from 9.14.0.0.0., or 452 A.D., to 9.15.-10.0.0., or 481 A.D. It would appear, therefore, that the city was occupied only for a period of about thirty years. Nakum, situated between Naranjo and Uaxactun, was probably founded about the same time. There are three sculptured stelæ at this site, in addition to twelve plain ones. The dates recorded on the sculptured stelæ are, 9.17.0.0.0., 511 A.D., 9.19.10.0.0., 56 A.D., and 10.-1.0.0.0., 590 A.D. Assuming that 10.1.0.0.0. was the last date at the city, which appears probable, and further that ten- and twenty-year periods were recorded, not in sculpture, but in painted stucco, upon the plain stelæ, then this would take us back to 9.14.0.0.0., or 452 A.D., as the date of the foundation of the city.

Ten years later, in 9.14.10.0.0., the city of Xultun was founded. It was occupied for a period of 170 years, up to 10.3.0.0.0., and was, with Uaxactun, the last city of their Old Empire to be deserted by the Maya.

In 9.15.0.0.0., or 471 A.D., we find the first dated monument at the great city of Quirigua, situated some 200 miles south of Uaxactun, in the Republic of Guatemala. The city consists of a great plaza, some 800 feet long by 200 feet broad, bounded to the south by an extensive group of temples, standing upon a lofty substructure, and to the north by a simple large temple also upon a substructure. Around this central core are grouped numerous buildings, mounds of ruins, and monuments, showing that the city must, at one time, have been fairly extensive. It is chiefly remarkable for the size and beauty of its stelæ and altars. One of the former projects for twenty-six feet from the earth, and one of the latter, sculptured in the form of a gigantic turtle, is the largest sculptured monolith in the Maya area. It also possesses the most complete set of five-year-period records known, some sculptured on the stelæ, others on the altars. They extend from 9.15.15.0.0., or 486 A.D., to 9.19.0.0.0., or 550 A.D., an unbroken period of sixty-five years.

La Honradez is a small site, situated some twenty-five miles to the northwest of Uaxactun, in the Peten district of Guatemala. There is only one sure date recorded here, 9.17.0.0.0., or 511 A.D., together with two doubtful ones, 9.18.0.0.0., 530 A.D., and 9.18.10.0.0., or 540 A.D. There are six stelæ at present undeciphered. Assuming that 9.18.10.0.0. is the last date recorded, the six undeciphered stelæ should take us back to 9.14.0.0.0., 452 A.D., for the foundation of the city.

Seibal is situated in the centre of the Peten district, some 100 miles southwest of Uaxactun. The dates deciphered here are, 9.16.0.0.0., 491 A.D., 9.17.0.0.0., 511 A.D., 9.18.0.0.0., 530 A.D., 9.18.10.0.0., 540 A.D., 10.1.0.0.0., 590 A.D., and 10.2.0.0.0., 609 A.D.

During the 5 Katuns, covering approximately a century, between 9.18.0.0.0., 530 A.D., and 10.3.0.0.0.,

629 A.D., a great number of small towns seem to have been founded throughout the Maya area. They are as follows: Ixkun, some 100 miles south of Uaxactun, where only one date, 9.18.0.0.0., has been deciphered. El Cayo, 145 miles southwest of Uaxactun, where one date only is recorded, 9.17.5.0.0., 516 A.D. Los Higos, where a single date also is found, 9.17.10.0.0. La Mar, within a few miles of El Cayo, where the dates 9.17.15.0.0., and 9.18.15.0.0. are recorded. Aguas Calientes, close to Altar de Sacrificios, where the single date, 9.18.0.0.0., is recorded. Cancuen, about forty-five miles south of Seibal, where two dates, 9.18.0.0.0. and 9.18.5.0.0., are recorded.

Chinkultic, almost due south of Palenque, was another small city dating from the end of the Old Empire. The earliest date recorded here is 9.17.10.0.0., the latest 10.0.15.0.0. The city was consequently occupied for a period of approximately sixty-five years.

Hatzcap Ceel, to the south of Benque Viejo, discovered by Mr. Eric Thompson in 1928, when the dates 9.19.0.0.0. and 10.0.5.0.0. were found on two altars. Ucanal, a few miles south of Benque Viejo, where the single date 10.1.0.0.0. is recorded.

Benque Viejo, near the boundary line between the western frontier of British Honduras and Guatemala, where the date 10.1.0.0.0. is recorded.

Flores, on Lake Peten Itza, in Guatemala, where the same date, 10.1.0.0.0., is recorded. Quen Santo, about 280 miles southwest of Uaxactun, in the extreme south-western corner of the Maya area, where two dates are recorded, 10.2.5.0.0. and 10.2.10.0.0.

Lastly, we have Chichen-Itza, in the north of Yucatan, where a single Initial Series date is recorded, 10.2.10.0.0., or 619 A.D.

The history of the Maya was formerly divided up into that of the Old and the New Empires, the former occupying the southern part of the Maya area, up to about the beginning of the seventh century A.D., the latter the peninsula of Yucatan, from that period on to the Spanish Conquest. Later research, however, has shown that this classification is inaccurate and misleading, as both Yucatan and the south were occupied simultaneously from very early times. The terms Old and New Empire are, however, still retained, as a matter of convenience, to designate, the latter, the Maya of Yucatan, the former, those of the rest of the Maya area.

The Maya area included the states of Chiapas and Tabasco in Mexico, the peninsula of Yucatan, Guatemala, Spanish Honduras, British Honduras, Salvador, and part of Nicaragua. Its extreme length from north to south is about 500 miles, and from east to west the same.

Uaxactun, the Maya's first settlement, was approximately in the centre of this area, and during the fifteen centuries which they occupied it, prior to the arrival of Europeans, they spread out over the entire area, founding more than 100 cities and towns, in every part of it.

The process of colonization was, however, rather a

remarkable one. The first city founded after Uaxactun was Tikal, in its immediate neighborhood, and situated on fertile land, which is quite as one would have expected. The next city, Copan, is no less than 300 miles to the south, at the very extreme southern limit of the Maya area, and the situation of the fourth city, Tuluum, 400 miles to the north, and situated on poor and unproductive soil, is still more incomprehensible.

After this, more than half the cities founded were situated within a circular area measuring about 100 miles in diameter, in the Peten district of Guatemala.

It is probable that many of the later cities were not colonized direct from Uaxactun, but from other cities which had been founded later in their neighborhood. Thus, Quirigua was almost certainly colonized from Copan, as was also, probably, Pusilhà. Hatzcap Ceel, Ucanal, and Benque Viejo appear to have been founded by emigrants from Naranjo, as were El Cayo and La Mar by emigrants from Yaxchilan. From Tuluum the Maya probably reached Cobà, and from the latter founded the great sacred city of Chichen-Itza, which later far outrivalled either of the older cities in importance.

The dozen, or so, small cities which were founded in the century between 9.18.0.0.0. and 10.3.0.0.0., the great majority of which were not occupied for more than twenty years, were almost certainly founded by immigrants from cities in their immediate vicinity, and curiously enough, the larger and older cities were al-

Plate V.   LINTEL 24 AT YAXCHILAN (MENCHÉ)

The kneeling penitent is engaged in making a sacrifice of blood by passing
a knotted cord with thorns through his tongue

After Maudslay

most all deserted before, or soon after, the rise of this mushroom crop of little towns, in the closing years of the Old Empire.

Doctor Morley has made a stylistic classification of the sculptured stelæ found in the Old Empire cities, into an Early Period, prior to 9.10.0.0.0., 373 A.D., a Middle Period, from 9.10.0.0.0. to 9.15.0.0.0., 471 A.D., and a Great Period, from 9.15.0.0.0. to the close of the Old Empire.

The earlier style is characterized by very low relief sculpture (and it is interesting to note that in the last degenerate days of the New Empire, the Maya reverted to their low relief), an irregularity of outline in the glyph blocks, an absence of ornament on the bars and dots of the numerals, a complexity of detail in the ornamentation of the glyphs, and a general crudeness and lack of technique in execution.

The styles, of course, merge gradually into one another, and allowance must be made for provincialism, and for backward towns, where the older technique lingered long after it had been superseded in the larger cities.

At Copan, this classification is particularly well exemplified. There, the stelæ may be divided into six classes:

1. Those with one face only sculptured.
2. Those with two alternate faces sculptured.
3. Stelæ, with glyphs on all four faces.

4. Those with glyphs on three sides.
5. Human figures on two sides, and glyphs on two
   sides.
6. A human figure on one side, its elaborate decorations occupying two sides, and glyphs on the
   back.

Now, of these six classes, the Early Period has examples of 1, 2, 3, and 4, the Middle Period of 3, 4,
and 5, and the Great Period of 4, 5, and 6.

Whether the Maya cities of the Old Empire were
bound together in some sort of a confederation or
league, analagous to the Greek cities, the Hanseatic
League, or the League of Mayapan of the New Empire, we do not know, but the probability seems to be
that they were, as warfare was practically unknown
amongst them, if one may judge by the almost complete absence of battle scenes, amongst those sculptured
on the monoliths and elsewhere. Moreover, a brisk
trade appears to have been carried on between all the
cities, throughout the entire Maya area, which could
not have been the case had internecine war been of frequent occurrence. It is difficult to conceive how such a
large number of small city states, treading on each
other's heels, as it were, especially around the central
part of the area, amongst which disputes must constantly have arisen over water, timber, agricultural and
hunting rights, can have preserved an unbroken peace,
over a period of at least six centuries, unless a single

ruler, or a central council, dominated the entire confederation, to whom such disputes were referred, and from whose decision there was no appeal.

Very interesting discoveries have been made recently by Mr. John Teeple, which throw considerable light on this subject. In studying the supplementary hieroglyphics, which almost invariably follow the dates, and deal with a lunar count, he found that, in the early period, which he calls the Period of Independence, there was a diversity in the method of writing these glyphs, which was followed by a Period of Unity, during which all the cities came into line, and finally a Period of Revolt, when each group of cities again reverted to independent methods in recording the lunar count. This would suggest that, for at least a considerable period, there was a general confederation of all the Maya city states.

Almost every city developed along lines of its own, and specialized in some particular activity.

Copan is celebrated for its exquisitely sculptured stelæ, Tikal for its beautiful wood carving, Quirigua for its wonderful Zoomorphic monuments, Palenque for its beautiful stucco mouldings and engraved jades, Pusilhà for its exquisite ceramics, Lubaantun for its figurines. There seems also to have been a wide distribution of the manufactures of each city. Engraved jades from Palenque are found as far west as Teotihuacan, near Mexico City, and as far north as Chichen-Itza. The beautiful painted pottery of Pusilhà is found in most of the neighboring cities, and the figurines of Lubaantun are found at least as far away as Naranjo.

During the century which elapsed between the end of Katun 18 of Bactun 9 and Katun 3 of Bactun 10, that is between 530 A.D. and 629 A.D., there occurred in the Old Empire perhaps one of the most remarkable events ever recorded in the history of any nation.

The entire population of all the cities deserted their homes in the south, with the enormous investment which these represented in temples, palaces, monoliths, and private houses, and migrated into the peninsula of Yucatan, where the soil was poor, and unsuited for the cultivation of maize, their staple foodstuff, and the water supply almost non-existent, owing to the absence of rivers and lagoons.

It was indeed very much as if the entire population of the towns in the English southern counties were suddenly, for no apparent reason, to migrate to the north of Scotland.

Though the great majority of the Maya trekked to Yucatan, a certain proportion migrated to the extreme west of Guatemala, where they founded the city of Quen Santo.

The sudden cessation in the erection of stelæ gives us almost the exact date at which each city was deserted.

The abandonment of the area as a whole was a gradual one, and occupied approximately a century. It commenced in the extreme south, at Copan, and in the extreme west at Palenque, extending thence eastward and northward, till it reached the cities of northeastern Peten, of which the group including Naranjo, Tikal, Uaxactun, Benque Viejo, and Nakum was the last to be deserted. The exodus from each city was, however, apparently a sudden one, as the last erected stelæ are almost in the best style of the Great Period, and show no signs of any degeneration in the sculptor's art.

A number of reasons have been assigned for this remarkable exodus, none of them, however, entirely satisfactory. They include:

1. National decadence.
2. Epidemic disease.
3. Earthquakes.
4. War, internecine or foreign, or both combined.
5. Climatic changes.
6. Exhaustion of the soil.
7. Religious, or superstitious reasons.

1. National Decadence

Spinden believes that the exodus was due to a moral and physical decadence, affecting the whole nation, of which the extraordinary exuberance and flamboyance of Maya art in its later stages was the index. But against this theory is the fact that there was no falling off in the style or technique of the stelæ, and indeed every city was apparently deserted at the time it had reached its artistic apogee. Furthermore, it would almost certainly have required a more cogent reason than this to force the entire population away from the homes of their ancestors, and the temples of their gods.

2. *Epidemic Disease*

There are only two possible diseases which may be considered in this connection, namely Malaria and Yellow Fever. The former is prevalent, often in a malignant form, over almost the whole Maya area, at the present day, yet has never, so far as I know, been the cause of the desertion of even a village much less a town. Furthermore, in the days of the Old Empire, the disease, if known at all, was probably far less prevalent than it is now, for the bush must have been entirely cleared over a vast area which is now forest, thus affording less harborage for the Anophiline mosquitoes, the carriers of the disease.

It has been stated that Yellow Fever originated in America, but we have no evidence in support of this assertion, and certainly none that it ever ravaged the Maya area.

3. *Earthquakes*

It will be noticed that in choosing sites for their cities, the Maya carefully avoided the earthquake zone. They built no farther south than Copan, and no farther east than Quirigua, probably for this reason. Their style of architecture was entirely unfitted to withstand earthquake shocks, and probably experience had taught them this, long before they erected their large cities.

Moreover, such a thing as the entire population of a large country deserting it in consequence of earthquake shocks is unknown in history, nor are there any signs left amongst the Maya cities of damage by earthquake. Such damage as has been effected is due, almost entirely, to the growth of a too-exuberant tropical vegetation.

4. War

The Maya, judging by the scenes depicted upon the stelæ, were one of the least warlike nations who ever existed. The only two sculptures which might suggest war are found at Piedras Negras. In one of these a number of naked captives are seen standing before a throne, upon which a ruler surrounded by attendants is seated. In the other, six warriors, armed with spears, kneel before a ruler, also bearing a spear.

The only enemies at all likely to have attacked the Maya were Nahua tribes coming in from the northwest. These, we know, did enter Central America, but they all followed the route along the Pacific side of the Continental Divide, while the Maya did not leave the Atlantic side, and so they never came in contact with each other. It is not impossible that an internecine warfare, say between the eastern and western cities, may have been, if not the sole, at least one of the contributory causes to the break-up of the Old Empire, and we know that the Maya of the New Empire, at the break-up of the League of Mayapan, did behave very much in this way.

The Xiu, though on the winning side during this bitter civil war, left their magnificent city of Uxmal, and wandered off into the bush, to the miserable village of Mani. The Itzas left their city of Chichen-Itza, and migrated to far off Peten, while the Cocoms deserted their city of Mayapan, and settled again at Sotuta.

5. Climatic Changes

Based on his observation of the giant Sequoia tree of California, Huntingdon believes that during the first millennium B.C., when the Maya first commenced to develop, there was a gradual improvement of the climate over the Maya area, which became drier and more bracing. Toward the end of the early period, and up to about 450 A.D., the climate again degenerated, and became much wetter and hotter. After this it again improved, and got drier, rendering it easier to keep down the bush. These conditions lasted for about a century, till the return of rainier conditions, about Katun 19, to be followed again by drier conditions, during Katun 1 and 2 of Bactun 10, coinciding with the last flare-up of the Old Empire civilization. Finally the climate became much hotter and wetter than it is to-day, resulting in the desertion of the entire area by its inhabitants, owing to the fact that, with the agricultural implements at their disposal, they were entirely unable to keep down the rapid forest growth.

This theory is at least interesting, and there exists a curious coincidence between Huntingdon's alternating favorable and unfavorable climatic conditions, and the periods of progress and retrogression in the Maya civilization.

6. *Exhaustion of the Soil*

The Maya mode of agriculture is probably much the same to-day as it was 2,000 years ago. It consists in felling a tract of virgin bush, burning the vegetation off, as soon as it has dried sufficiently in the sun, and then planting the area with corn. This area is allowed to lie fallow for from two to six years, when the same procedure is repeated. At every planting the soil becomes poorer, and the crop smaller, till at length the area becomes covered with coarse grass, and is useless for agricultural purposes.

This is not impossibly what took place at the larger Maya cities, till they became at last islets in a vast green sea of grass, and the inhabitants were compelled to go so far afield for land suitable for cultivation, that they were constrained to leave these densely populated centres and seek pastures new.

7. *Religious and Superstitious Reasons*

The Maya were an intensely religious people. Every act of their daily lives was motived by religious considerations, and it is possible that, finding their food supply failing them, year after year, they began to lose confidence in their gods, and in the priests, their servants and ministers, till at length these were compelled to proclaim a general exodus, by divine command, in order to retain their own influence.

Those cities which were ill situated, from an agricultural point of view, would naturally be the first deserted, while the cities in the fertile lands of northeastern Peten would be amongst the last.

Whatever the cause, it is certain that by the third Katun of Bactun 10, or 629 A.D., the whole of the Old Empire was almost completely abandoned, and remained so for the next seven or eight centuries, when reforestation of the lands enabled at least a part of the descendants of the original dwellers to return to the home of their ancestors.

CHAPTER III

THE HISTORY OF YUCATAN
(J. E. T.)

Chols and Chortis may have been the original Mayas. Causes which led the Maya to migrate to Yucatan. Evidence afforded by Cobà and the ruins along the eastern coast of Yucatan. The Chilam Balaam of Chumayel, giving the history of the Itzas. The Chilam Balaams of Mani and Tizimin give accounts of the Xius, the other royal family of Yucatan. The founding of Chichen-Itza and its first period of occupancy. Number of monuments no criterion as to length of occupancy of a city. Chichen-Itza abandoned by the Itza, who go to Champoton. The coming of the Xius, who drive the Itzas from Champoton. Return of the Itzas to Chichen-Itza. The arrival of the great hero god and leader, Kukulcan. The Xius found the city of Uxmal. Formation of League of Mayapan between the Zius, the Itzas and the Cocoms. The Cocoms of Mayapan, with the aid of Mexican mercenaries, seize the rulership of Yucatan. They are finally driven out and nearly the whole family massacred. The war was followed by a period of great prosperity. This was succeeded by a terrific hurricane and a fatal epidemic, after which civil war broke out, which continued up to the Conquest. The first arrival of the Spaniards. The coming of Montejo, who was assisted by the Xius. The Spaniards are driven from Yucatan. The massacre of the Xius by the Cocoms. Second Spanish invasion, in 1540, is successful. Ill treatment of the Indians by their conquerors. The war of the castes, and why the Indians failed to regain their liberty.

In endeavoring to trace out the history of Yucatan during its occupation by the Mayas, we are forced to wander along trails and blind paths that appear to meander aimlessly through the swamps of uncertainty and lack of precise information. Dated stelæ, those handy signposts that have marked the path with such accuracy in the period of the "Old Empire" in the southern region, are in Yucatan almost entirely lacking except for the first period. Which of these trails, that appear to start and end nowhere, should be followed is the problem that faces anyone who undertakes to act as guide through the morass.

The scraps of evidence, to drop the metaphor, are in many cases conflicting, and to attempt a reasonable reconstruction of Yucatecan history at this moment one must be prepared to ignore evidence which the future may well reveal as worthy of full credence. The time has not yet come when an accurate and scientific outline of the events that occurred in Yucatan prior to the arrival of the Spaniards can be made. Much excavation and examination of unpublished records will be necessary before we can be sure of our ground. This short outline of Yucatecan history must, therefore, be taken as being to a large extent tentative.

The writer believes, although at the present time there is no definite proof, that the Old Empire region of the Peten, and the area to the south, was originally occupied by the Chols, and that they were responsible for the development of the distinctive Maya civilization. The Chols were a people speaking a dialect of the Maya language, not very different from that now spoken in Yucatan. Indeed, the remnants of the Chol people, with the closely allied Chortis, still occupy the whole of the southern region of the Old Empire.

Be this as it may, shortly before the close of the

PLATE VI.   LABNA: TYPICAL YUCATAN ARCHITECTURE

Note the human face in the open jaws of the conventionalized snake, and
the thin façade stones

early period (circa 350 A.D.) some of the inhabitants
of the Peten region, who had gradually been expanding
in a northeasterly direction, reached the eastern part of
Yucatan.

Possibly this colonization was due to the pressure of
an increasing population, but perhaps it would be
simpler to attribute it to the urge of expansion of a
virile people, ever in search of new forest lands to fell
for their maize fields. At this time Maya culture was
gathering momentum, pullulating with the energy that
was to flourish in the great period. It was a period that
might be compared to the Elizabethan age in England
when a great wave of activity, both mental and physical,
swept over the country.

Whatever the cause may have been, as early as 353
A.D. (9.9.0.0.0.) the immigrants were firmly established
around Lake Cobà, in eastern Yucatan, Tuluum on the
coast, and Ichpaatun to the south on the shores of Chetemal Bay, where Doctor Gann discovered a stela dated
9.8.0.0.0., 5 Ahau 3 Chen (333 A.D.)

At Macanxoc, close to Cobà, and Cobà itself no less
than fourteen sculptured stelæ have been found. These
are of very great beauty, worthy of the best Maya traditions, although the cities were far removed from the
centre of Maya culture. Most of the monuments represent priests or deities standing on bound captives,
doubtless victims, who were to be sacrificed when the
stelæ were erected. The grouping of these captives is
particularly fine. The sculpture is in a style that bears a

strong resemblance to that of the monuments being erected about this time at Naranjo and other sites of the central and northern Peten. Furthermore the architecture of the principal buildings and the method of grouping them at Cobà, and at the site of Kucican, some ten miles to the south, are very similar to those obtaining in the northern Peten. For instance there is a peculiar development of the vaulted arch at Uaxactun. This takes the form of a series of insets, instead of the usual inward slope, the whole effect being not unlike a pair of inverted staircases. This same development occurs also at Cobà.

In short, sufficient evidence can be produced to show that this culture that flourished along the eastern coast of Yucatan and its hinterland was directly inspired from the Peten region. However, there was one local development that seems to have originated without any inspiration from the south—the great paved causeways described by Doctor Gann in chapter II. Up to the present nothing analogous has been reported from the Peten or the region to the south, and we are forced to conclude that these great stone roads originated in this area.

These colonists in eastern Yucatan were not, in all probability, Yucatan's first inhabitants. Western Yucatan was probably already peopled by the Yucatecan Mayas, the same race that still exists all over the northern half of the peninsula, and whom the Spaniards found in control of the country on their first arrival in 1517.

We can picture this people as already settled in this region, and possessed of a developed local culture. They would have inherited the common basis of all Maya culture, the roots of which must have tapped the pre-Maya culture, that was spread over the whole middle American highland region from the Valley of Mexico to El Salvador.

One gets the picture of this local civilization developing in Yucatan, influenced to a certain extent by the culture of the Peten and, to a greater extent, by that of the region around the mouth of the Usamacintla River in Tabasco. At this time the seeds must have been sown of that local architecture, which later was to blossom forth into the florid style, typical of Uxmal, Chichen-Itza, and the other cities of western Yucatan—an architecture which might almost be styled Maya rococo.

Possibly in the fifth or sixth centuries the Peten culture in eastern Yucatan was absorbed by that of the Yucatecan Mayas, after it, in turn, had first modified the dominant culture. The difference in language would not have been a serious barrier against the amalgamation of the two peoples, if the colonists of eastern Yucatan were, indeed, Chols, for the Chols spoke a language closely allied to Yucatecan Maya. There are in existence about half a dozen books known as the books of the jaguar soothsayers (Chilam Balaam). These books contain a mixed assortment of medical lore, title deeds, family records, and Maya history. Parts of these books were, it appears pretty certain, originally in the form of hieroglyphic codices. However, shortly after the Spanish Conquest, they were reduced to writing by Mayas, who, having been educated by the Catholic priests, had learned to write Maya with our European characters. Unfortunately the historical information they contain is both scrappy and confused.

The most important of these ancient native histories is that contained in the Chilam Balaam of Chumayel. Chumayel is a small town in western Yucatan where these books reposed, in the keeping of Maya families, until brought to light by Yucatecan historians in the nineteenth century. The Chumayel books give an outline of the history of the Itzas, one of the three chief reigning families of Yucatan, and for a long time actual rulers of Chichen-Itza. In fact the name Chichen-Itza means "The mouth of the well of the Itzas." The word *Itza* also means "Holy," and, actually, the Itzas seem to have been the religious leaders of the northern part of the peninsula. The Chilam Balaam of Mani and Tizimin, on the other hand, recount the history of the chief rivals of the Itzas, the Xiu, who eventually became the rulers of Uxmal, and, for a short period, of the whole of northern Yucatan.

The Itzas were, possibly, of that Peten stock that settled in eastern Yucatan. From Cobà some of these colonists undoubtedly migrated west and founded the city of Yaxhuna about the middle of cycle nine (350 A.D.). This site lies about ten miles south of Chichen-Itza, and although no dated monuments have been found there, there is no doubt that it was occupied at an early period. Here the great causeway that stretches westward from Cobà terminates. The evidence is too lengthy to be given here, but there is no doubt that these causeways date from the middle of cycle nine. After Yaxhuna had been occupied, possibly for 100 years, Chichen-Itza was settled.

The Maya chronicles, translated from the brief concrete ideas of the hieroglyphs, laconically report its settlement in these few words: "6 Ahau (9.14.0.0.0., 452 A.D.) Chichen-Itza was discovered." Originally this was probably written in three glyphs. One for the date 6 Ahau, a second the name glyph of the city, and a third for settlement or discovery.

Chichen-Itza was an ideal spot for settlement, as three large "cenotes" insured a plentiful supply of water in this waterless country. *Cenote* is a word derived from the Maya *dzonot* used to describe large natural wells caused by the caving in of the earth's crust above the subterranean lakes and rivers which abound in Yucatan. They are found scattered all over the northern half of the peninsula, and are often of great size. The sacred cenote at Chichen-Itza, where in later times human sacrifice to the water deities took place, has a diameter of close on 150 feet, and the water, the surface of which is some sixty feet below the level of the ground, is in turn nearly sixty feet deep.

The earliest settlement at Chichen-Itza appears to have been to the south of what is now the centre of the city. No buildings survive, so far as we know, from this time, when the city was first occupied at the close of the fifth century. However, there are a number of buildings that probably date from the sixth century. By this time the Peten style of architecture has been largely replaced by a composite style. The massive, but roughly dressed stone façades of the Peten style have given place to façades composed of shallow evenly cut stones, smoothed level on the front, which form a veneer to the concrete-like mass of the walls of the buildings. The masks of the rain gods with their long curling snouts, which had been modelled in stucco in the Peten culture area, are now carved on stones, which like a mosaic pattern are fitted together in position on the façades of buildings. (Plate VII.)

This first occupation of Chichen-Itza by the Itzas lasted 220 years, and during this long interval the city must have grown from its very humble birth to magnificent size. This first occupation of the city is interesting in that it shows the fallacy of the theory so often advanced that the length of occupation of a city is shown by the monuments erected there. During these 220 years only one monument with a fixed date in the Maya long count is known to have been erected (a lintel giving the date 10.2.10.0.0., 2 Ahau 13 Chen, 619 A.D.). Nevertheless the Chilam Balaam give the duration of this period as 11 Katuns (220 years). Shortly after 650 A.D. Chichen-Itza was suddenly abandoned by its inhabitants. No reason is assigned for this desertion of the

The "Iglesia," a one-room temple of the pre-Mexican period with elaborate façade with masks of the rain god

East end of the "Monjas." The stone door lintel has a hieroglyphic inscription

PLATE VII. CHICHEN–ITZA

temples and palaces that represented the wealth accumulated over so long a period by the community. One might hazard the opinion that it was due to religious reasons. Possibly an oracle decreed that the city was to be abandoned, or possibly the soil was becoming exhausted and needed a period of rest in order to yield once more a full crop. There is, however, a more plausible explanation.

At this time great movements of peoples were taking place to the south. The cities of the Peten and the south had recently ceased to function as religious centres. The erection of new monuments and temples had ceased, and a period of uncertainty and unrest had set in. Such events could not have failed to have repercussions in Yucatan, and may have influenced the Itzas in their decision to abandon their capital. One very direct result of this upheaval to the south was the arrival of the Xius in Yucatan. The Xius wasted little time in starting a quarrel with the Itzas. A quarrel, moreover, that was to endure until the arrival of the Spaniards.

Forty years after abandoning Chichen-Itza, the Itzas established themselves at Champoton (known to the Mayas as Chakanputun), situated on the west coast of Yucatan in the centre of the State of Campeche. Within some twenty years of this, the Xius had established themselves in the vicinity of the Lake of Bakhalal, on the east coast of Yucatan close to Chetemal Bay, and probably not far from the city of Tzibanche, discovered by Doctor Gann in 1927.

The Xius seem to have been of Maya stock, and pos-sibly came from the Chiapas-South Tabasco area. The Yucatecans referred to them as foreigners, a term the Xius resented bitterly, and tried to show their Yuca-tecan standing in later times by being more patriotic than the real Yucatecan, just as a naturalized citizen of a country is usually more patriotic or jingoistic than the native-born inhabitant. The word *Xiu* is possibly Mexi-can in origin; however, the Xius probably got their name from their Mexican neighbors in their original home.

The Xius seem to have resided only forty years on the shores of Bakhalal, for in 10.10.0.0.0. they occupied Chichen-Itza, which had now been unoccupied for a century since its abandonment by the Itzas, who were still settled at Champoton. However, that restlessness that characterized the Mayas in their past (as indeed it does at the present time), urging them ever to move, soon caused the Xius to abandon Chichen-Itza once again. In 10.16.0.0.0., 120 years after their arrival at Chichen-Itza they moved to the east coast, in the tracks of the Itzas. The accounts are somewhat confused as to what exactly happened when the Xius arrived at Cham-poton. They may have seized the city straight away from the Itzas, but it rather looks as though they set-tled down alongside the Itzas for sixty years, pre-sumably in peace. At the end of that period in 10.19.-0.0.0., they seized Champoton from the Itzas and ex-pelled them from the country. Like the Jews in the Old

Testament the Itzas wandered forty years in the wilderness. "In this Katun," the chronicle narrates, "those of Itza were under the trees, under the boughs, under the branches, to their sorrow; . . . two score years (they had resided at Champoton) when they came and established their houses a second time, and they lost Chakanputun." The expression about establishing their houses a second time refers to the return which the Itzas now made to Chichen-Itza.

Shortly after the return of the Itzas to their old capital, Mexican influences would appear to have first made themselves felt in Yucatan.

In the middle of the thirteenth century lived a remarkable man, who profoundly influenced the history of the whole of Central America. He was known to the Mexicans as Quetzalcoatl, but the Mayas called him Kukulcan. Actually the name has practically the same significance in both languages, meaning in Mexican "Quetzal-bird-serpent," in Maya "feathered serpent." Kukulcan, as he will be called in this book, was named for the feathered serpent god, patron of the dawn and the dawn wind and god of the planet Venus. Kukulcan, who was a Toltec ruler, would appear to have first reached Chichen-Itza as a prisoner of war. It would seem that he was destined to be sacrificed as an offering to the rain deities. At Chichen, victims were sacrificed to obtain rain by being cast alive into the deep sacred well. The victim, clad in all his finery, was hurled down to the water sixty feet below, at dawn. At mid-day, if he were still alive, he was hauled out and raised to the highest rank, as it was believed that the rain deities had expressed a desire that the victim should live, and, as he had taken divine rank on being offered as a sacrifice, he now became a living god on earth. The evidence for this having been the fate of Kukulcan is not very strong, but it is by no means unlikely.

Whether this story is true or not, Kukulcan became the ruler of Chichen-Itza, and the most powerful chief in Yucatan. He founded the city of Mayapan, which he made the civil capital of the peninsula, although Chichen-Itza continued to be the religious centre. He organized the whole peninsula into one state, and caused the chiefs of the different areas to take up residence in Mayapan. He also brought over mercenaries from Mexico to keep the peace. Since he had been granted divine rank by his return to this world from the realm of the rain gods and secondly had proved himself such an able organizer, his worship became very widespread. A great architectural period set in inspired by this cultural renaissance, and a feverish activity in building ensued. The temples and palaces of this period and the ensuing two centuries are easily distinguishable by their use of the feathered serpent motif, the symbol of Kukulcan. Under the impetus of this renaissance new architectural details were employed. Many of these were not actually new, having been employed in other cities previously, but they were new to the Itzas. Columns came to be extensively used, and they, combined with wide wooden lintels, allowed of the erection of temples with rooms of a size hitherto impossible. It has been suggested that many of these architectural details were of Mexican origin. However, although some may well have been derived from this source, the majority were probably developed locally.

Kukulcan appears to have been responsible for the introduction from Mexico of round temples such as the "Caracol" at Chichen-Itza and the circular temple at Mayapan.

A few years before the appearance of Kukulcan in Yucatan the Xius, under their leader Ah Cuitok Tutul Xiu, founded the city of Uxmal. Kukulcan either conquered the Xius or made an alliance with them. The Xius by this time had become the second most important people in Yucatan, and probably would have become the dominant force in the peninsula at this time had not Kukulcan appeared on the scene.

Kukulcan, after pacifying Yucatan, and establishing a strong central government at Mayapan, left Yucatan. He next appears in Tabasco, where, with the aid of twenty chiefs, he overran the country, and added it to his empire. Whether he returned to his native Mexico after this is uncertain, as we have no information as to where he died.

During the 200 years that followed the departure of Kukulcan, Yucatan was at peace. The three chief cities, Chichen-Itza, Mayapan, and Uxmal, appear to have formed a league and to have jointly governed the country. Possibly Itzamal, another important Itza city, was admitted to this league as a joint ruler. The rulers of Mayapan were the Cocoms. The Cocoms seem to have been instituted as governors on the departure of Kukulcan. Gradually, during the succeeding two centuries, the power and authority of the Cocoms increased, and the triple alliance was slowly transformed into a Cocom tyranny. The oppressive measures of the Cocoms were deeply resented by the other Mayas and in particular by the Xius of Uxmal. Apparently attempts were made to cast off the yoke of the Cocoms, but the attempts failed, and the Cocoms called in Mexican mercenaries to insure that no further attempts would succeed. Thus for the second time Mexicans came to Yucatan, for it will be recalled Kukulcan had introduced Mexicans into the country 200 years earlier. It is not known from what part of Mexico these mercenaries were brought, but we should probably not be far wrong in hazarding that their homes were situated in the Vera Cruz region bordering on Tlaxcalla.

Despite the arrival of these Mexicans warfare broke out. The ruler of Chichen-Itza at this time was Chac Xib Chac, "The red man." He seems to have concocted a plot with the ruler of Itzamal, a certain Ulil, to rise in rebellion against the tyranny of Mayapan. Legend says that the fighting started because Chac Xib Chac stole the bride of the ruler of Mayapan, but this is probably a later romantic coloring. The casus belli was a banquet which Chac Xib Chac gave to Ulil. Presumably this was to have been the cementing of the alliance and an occasion for working out in detail the arrangements for the revolt. However, Hunac Ceel, the ruler of Mayapan and presumably, therefore, one of the Cocom family, heard of this meeting of the two rulers. He seems to have been determined to nip the plot in the bud and strike before his enemies' plans were mature. Assisted by his Mexican allies under the leadership of seven chiefs, Hunac Ceel fell on Chichen-Itza and utterly routed the inhabitants. However, despite this signal victory the other leaders of Yucatan under the leadership of the Xius continued the war against the city of Mayapan, and its governor, Hunac Ceel, the people of Itzamal also taking a leading part in the fighting, which culminated in the destruction of Mayapan, the death of Hunac Ceel, the murder of the Cocom family, and the disarming of the Mexican mercenaries. The date of the destruction of Mayapan is one of the few uncontroverted facts given by the native sources, the year being 1451 A.D., exactly ninety years before the final conquest of the country by the Spaniards.

The close of what might be termed "the war of independence" was followed by one of those periods of wholesale migration which, we have seen, characterized Maya civilization. The Itza rulers abandoned Chichen-Itza, and migrated south into the Peten. There they established themselves on the islands in the middle of the lake now known as Flores. They seem to have concluded an alliance with the Mopan Mayas, who had probably migrated south from Yucatan at an earlier date, and they also lived on friendly terms with the Chols to the south and southwest of them. It will be remembered that it was suggested earlier in the chapter that the Chols were the immigrants who first settled eastern Yucatan, and might be the ancestors of the Itzas. If that were indeed the case, the Itzas would have returned to their ancestral homes, and come again to be among their own people, though a people whose language they had now lost.

The Xius, in turn, abandoned their old capital, Uxmal, with its magnificent temples and stately palaces, and moved to Mani, where the task of erecting new edifices and the building of a new city awaited them. Exhausted by the war, they never succeeded, and Mani to-day is a small unimportant village, where little or no traces of the pre-conquest period survive. However, the Xiu family seem to have fallen heirs to the city of Chichen-Itza, which, despite the departure of its rulers, the Itza family, would appear never to have been entirely abandoned.

Of the whole Cocom family there was only one survivor of the massacre that marked the close of the war —a massacre that must have exceeded in barbarity that of the Royal family in Russia, and one, too, justified on the same grounds of tyranny and oppression. This lucky survivor owed his life to the fact that he had been absent on a visit to another part of the country when his father and the rest of the family were slain. Returning to his people, he gathered as many as would follow him, and moving over to the northeast coast of the peninsula settled at a spot he named "Tibulon," which means "We were judged," apparently an allusion to the overthrow of his family owing to their tyranny. The people gradually increased in numbers and power, and by the time the Spaniards reached Yucatan, the Cocoms were once more a powerful people. They do not appear ever to have forgiven their old enemies. With the Chels who were the governors of Itzamal and Zizontun they maintained a perpetual feud. They controlled the salt deposits on the coast, and refused to allow the Chels to send there to gather salt. The Chels replied by forbidding the export to Cocom territory of cacao beans and other fruit grown in their own land.

The allies seem to have treated very leniently the Mexican mercenaries, who assisted Hunac Ceel against them, for they permitted the Mexicans to settle in Yucatan, alloting them special territory, only making the stipulation that they should not intermarry with the Yucatecans.

The war was followed by twenty years of abundance, during which the country had time to recover from its devastating effects. Nevertheless, central government had disappeared with the destruction of Mayapan, although the Xiu family seem to have made an unsuccessful attempt to take the place of the Cocom family as rulers of the whole of Yucatan. Yucatan was now divided into half a dozen important principalities, each ruled over by its own chief, and in addition there were possibly a dozen further minor chiefs, who ruled over small areas. The country was only unified religiously.

Yucatan was just getting on its feet again when the country was swept by a terrible hurricane, which did incalculable harm, destroying the crops and fruit trees. This was followed fifteen years later by a series of plagues, under which the natives died like flies. To make things worse civil war broke out, and continued intermittently until the final subjugation of the country by the Spaniards. In fact the relative ease with which the Spaniards were enabled to conquer the country was due to these two factors—dissension and disease.

The first contact between Spaniards and Yucatecans occurred in 1511, nineteen years after the discovery of the new world by Columbus. The first round of the fight certainly went to the Mayas. A schooner returning from the mainland north of Panama was wrecked off the coast of Jamaica. The survivors in a small rowboat drifted to the east coast of Yucatan, where they fell into the hands of a small Maya chief. Several of them were promptly sacrificed, but two of the survivors escaped from the wooden cages in which prisoners were kept pending sacrifice, and fled into the territory of neighboring chiefs. One of these, Geronimo Aguilar, spent eight years among the Mayas, first as a slave and later as a counsellor to the local chief. In 1519 Cortes

Chichen-Itza: The "Castillo" reputed to have been built by Kukulcan. The photograph shows the restoration being carried out by the Mexican Government.

Uxmal: Elaborate façade decoration.   The lower part has fallen.

PLATE VIII

put in at Cozumel on his way to Mexico, and hearing that there were Spaniards captive among the Mayas sent messages telling them to come to him. Aguilar made his way to Cortes and was warmly welcomed. Thanks to his enforced residence among the Maya, he could, naturally, speak their language perfectly, and for that reason was of great service to Cortes as an interpreter. The other prisoner, a sailor by the name of Gonzalo Guerrero, also gained his freedom, becoming military advisor to the local chief. He married a Maya woman, and adopted the customs of the country, having his face tattooed and his ears pierced for the insertion of ornaments. When he received Cortes' message he refused to return, and definitely threw in his lot with the natives. In later years he organized the Maya resistance in the Chetemal area against the Spaniards, and according to one account died fighting against the Spanish invaders. Needless to say he was cordially detested by the Spaniards, who considered him an unspeakable traitor and idolator.

The actual discovery of Yucatan took place, as a matter of fact, two years before the arrival of Cortes. In 1517, Francisco Hernandez de Cordoba sailed round the coast, making landings at Isla de Mujeres, Cabo Catoche, Campeche and Champoton. The Spaniards had a hot welcome at Champoton. Over twenty of them were killed, two were taken prisoners and sacrificed, and Francisco Hernandez himself received no less than thirty-three wounds. He returned to Cuba with news of his discoveries and exaggerated reports of the wealth of the country based on the small gold trinkets he had been given by the natives.

The first actual attempt to conquer and settle the country was made by Francisco Montejo, who, on hearing news of the discovery of Yucatan, hurried to Sevilla, and got himself appointed "Adelantado" of the new land. His next step was a wise one. He married a rich widow, who supplied the money to fit out the expedition. The invaders landed at Cozumel, where they were received in peace. Later he passed into the territory of the Chels, where also he was well received. The Chels conceded Montejo permission to make a settlement at Chichen-Itza, and thither the Spaniards moved. Montejo seems to have acted in a very unmilitary way. He calmly settled down in the centre of a hostile country, where he could be cut off with ease from his supplies and any possible re-inforcements, and where, should he be forced to retreat, he would have no safe line along which to retire. This is what actually happened. At first all went well. The Xius, seeing an opportunity of scoring off some of their enemies, made an alliance with the Spaniards, and fought on their side against their fellow Yucatecans. The Chels remained neutral, consequently Montejo was able to subdue the country as he advanced. He proceeded to divide the country up among his followers and to impose tribute on the Indians. The result was a determined effort by the Indians to drive him out. He was besieged in Chichen-Itza, and only escaped by a subterfuge. With his troops Montejo escaped back to the north coast where the Chels still remained friendly. From there he crossed overland again with the help of the Chels, to Campeche, and thence to Mexico. Thus the first attempt to pacify Yucatan failed utterly.

During the interval that elapsed between the first invasion and the second Yucatan suffered from a severe drought. The custom existed among the Mayas of sacrificing a victim to the rain gods during periods of prolonged drought. This ceremony was observed with great ceremony at Chichen-Itza, where the victim was thrown into one of the "cenotes." The Xius, in the face of the severe drought, decided to make a pilgrimage to Chichen-Itza, and sacrifice slaves to bring rain. They sent an embassy to their enemies the Cocoms stating their intentions, and requesting a safe conduct through the Cocom territory. The Cocoms agreed to this, but when the Xius entered their territory, they set fire to the house in which the Xius were lodged, killing them as they tried to escape the flames. In many ways one can not help sympathizing with the Cocoms. The Xius, their hereditary enemies, had sided with the Spaniards against their fellow countrymen. The Xius were foreigners, but were for ever expressing their patriotism, yet when invaders from outside came to enslave the Mayas, the Xius allied themselves with them. The conquest of the country was inevitable, yet had the Xius not joined forces with the Spaniards the conquest might at least have been averted for another half century.

More civil war followed this massacre of the Xius, and the country was afflicted by swarms of locusts. Consequently, when the Spanish invasion was repeated in 1540, the country was quickly conquered. In 1541 resistance was at an end and the Spaniards were able to set up their capital at Merida on the ruins of the Maya city of Tiho. The country and its inhabitants were divided up among the invaders, and a period of barbarism and cruelty was ushered in. Sporadic revolts were ruthlessly crushed, and even Bishop Landa, who himself was not over squeamish, protests in his book of the horrors perpetrated. He writes of chiefs burnt alive and others hanged; of Chels, to whom the Spaniards owed their lives during the first invasion, being shut up in a house which was subsequently set on fire; of women and children hanged from the branches of a great tree; of prisoners whose hands, arms or legs were cut off; and lastly, of women being drowned by being thrown into deep lakes with weights on their feet. These cruelties were excused in the name of religion and on the grounds of fear of the overwhelming numbers of natives. The commands of God to the children of Israel to slay their enemies without mercy were cited as divine sanction for these atrocities.

Despite the conquest of Yucatan and that of the Maya peoples in Guatemala by Alvarado the cruel, the old Maya culture continued to flourish, or at least to exist, among the Itzas established in their island home in the Peten. Ta Itzal, "the place of the Itzas," continued to bear the standard of Maya civilization for another century and a half, although the waves of Spanish cruelty and avarice were for ever dashing themselves against the little island in the name of the God of mercy and love. The final subjection of the Itzas took place in 1702. Ta Itzal was destroyed and the remnants of the Itzas, after being robbed of all their possessions and receiving the sacrament of holy baptism, were scattered over the face of the surrounding country. At the present time their descendants pass a miserable existence in four or five scattered villages, ignorant of their great past and content to slave for their conquerors, gathering chewing gum for the delectation of Chicago's stenographers and drug-store clerks.

After the first sporadic uprisings against the Spaniards had been ruthlessly suppressed, Yucatan settled down to three centuries of superficial peace. Smallpox, in the early days, had decimated the Mayas, but gradually their numbers increased again, despite the ravages of two other diseases introduced by the Spaniards —malaria and hookworm. Conditions during the period were terrible. The Mayas were slaves in all but name. The big Spanish plantation owners kept their Maya laborers always in debt, and owned them body and soul. In the middle of the nineteenth century the Mayas, for the first time in three centuries, found themselves in possession of both arms and leaders. They had, very foolishly from the Spanish point of view, been armed to take part in some Mexican revolution, and after the fighting had succeeded in retaining their weapons. The Maya leaders were Felipe Pat and Cecilio Chi, two brave and intelligent men. The Mayas of Yucatan, in the face of continuous persecution and ill treatment, rose in arms. In a short while Valladolid and the whole of Yucatan except Merida was in their hands. Merida, however, was being besieged. The whites and half-castes shut up in the city appealed to the United States for help, promising to put themselves under American protection in return, but the American appetite for alien territory was, for the moment, assuaged and the offer was turned down. Victory was within the grasp of Pat and Chi, but they had a force stronger than the Yucatecan army with which to contend. The call of the soil, which had sounded in Maya ears for at least a couple of thousand years, was too strong to be resisted. The Maya army melted away, as man after man and group after group stole away to answer the call. The panic-stricken whites and half-castes were saved, and plucking up their courage took the offensive and drove back the depleted Maya ranks. Soon Yucatan was once more in white hands and the last chance of independence was lost. The defeated Mayas were struck down, captured and sold into indentured slavery in Cuba. Many of the Mayas retreated to the east coast of the peninsula, where they kept up the war, on and off, for another half century.

The only European race besides the Spaniards with whom the Mayas have been in contact is the British.

From early times the Mayas and British have been close friends, except in 1872, when one of the independent Maya chieftains of southern Yucatan declared war on Great Britain and invaded British Honduras. During the war of the castes, as the rising against the whites in Yucatan is called, the English helped the Mayas, supplying them with arms and ammunition. During the world war of 1914–1918 the Mayas paid back their debt, for in the ranks of the contingent of the British army recruited in British Honduras were several volunteers with Maya blood in their veins. One of these rose to be a sergeant-major in Mesopotamia.

In Guatemala many Mayas of the Quiche and other tribes have risen to positions of importance and many of Guatemala's presidents have had Maya blood in their veins. The Maya race is stubborn and will not die out. The Mayas with a tincture of European blood, with a Latin culture, and with a Latin outlook on religion, will continue to be the dominant stock in the lands where their culture first blossomed and came to maturity.

CHAPTER IV

ART AND ARCHITECTURE
(T. G.)

Maya architecture. Handicapped by the ignorance of the principle of the true arch. Two methods of roofing only available. The false, or cantilever, arch and its disadvantages. Use of the lofty entablature and roof comb for decorative purposes. All Maya buildings of any importance stood on truncated pyramids, usually terraced, and faced with cut stone. Development of Maya architecture. Construction of private houses. Objects aimed at by the Maya in the construction of their temples. Maya sculpture, the stone used, and the tools. Development of sculpture. Conventionalism of Maya art. Influence of religion upon it. Maya paintings. The colors used. Paintings upon paper, stucco, and pottery. The potter's art. Absence of the wheel throughout aboriginal America. Methods of fabricating and decorating pottery vessels. Maya textiles of the Old and New Empires. Colored designs and feather work ornamented the early Maya fabrics. Spinning and weaving. Basketry. Metal work of the New Empire. In the Old Empire metals were not used. Flint and obsidian chipping. Jade carving.

In the construction of stone buildings the Maya architects were greatly handicapped by their ignorance of the principle of the true arch. Two methods of roofing only were available for them, either beams placed across the walls or supported on pillars, or the false arch. The vast majority of the buildings in the Old Empire were connected with religion, and for these the false arch was invariably employed.

Later, the beamed roof was largely used, especially in the construction of private houses, few of which, unfortunately, have survived, owing to the decay of the wood of which the beams were made and the consequent caving in of the roof.

The false or cantilever arch was constructed in the following manner. When the side walls of the building reached the desired height, usually six to twelve feet, their inner faces were brought together by means of overlapping courses, like two inverted stairways placed opposite each other. When only a small interval was left at the top this was covered over with flat flags of stone.

The disadvantage of this form of arch is that, unlike the true arch, where each stone is self-supporting, the weight of each course has to be carried by the one beneath it, in consequence of which a great mass of solid masonry is required in the walls of the building, to act as counterpoise to the outward thrust of the arch. A further disadvantage is that the breadth of the chamber is necessarily limited to the span of the arch, which with the masonry used by the Maya could never exceed eighteen feet. In buildings constructed along these lines the room space is about equalled, and in some cases considerably exceeded, by the solid masonry necessary to contain it. The walls of Maya buildings were composed of rubble and mortar, covered externally by a mosaic of small rectangular stones.

The false arch must of necessity spring from the chamber walls at a very obtuse angle, and this gave rise to a lofty and almost perpendicular entablature on the exterior of the building, offering an ideal place for decoration. This space was taken full advantage of by the Maya architect, who extended it further by the erection of a lofty roof comb, which was sometimes solid, sometimes a series of narrow false-arched chambers. The space thus afforded was ornamented in a variety of ways, sometimes, as at Palenque, by covering it with moulded painted stucco, or, as in Yucatan, with sculpture in low relief, executed on a mosaic of small stones.

Practically all Maya buildings stood upon truncated pyramids, varying from two to 180 feet in height. The larger of these pyramids were terraced, the bounding walls usually possessing a well-marked batter. The angles were square in the earlier pyramids, but frequently rounded in the later ones. The substructures were built of earth and rubble, or sometimes of large blocks of stone and loose mortar. They were usually faced with squared stone, and were approached by steep stone stairways, sometimes on one side only, but in the larger pyramids on all four faces.

But a single building containing more than one story is known in the entire Maya area; a small three-storied square temple in the palace at Palenque. In many instances, however, the most notable example perhaps being the structure known as the Monjas at Chichen-Itza, buildings are constructed at various levels upon the sides of a solid, stepped pyramidal core, which give the impression of a two- or three-storied erection.

The Maya architect started with a single-roomed

Plate IX. GATEWAY AT LABNA

structure, having one rectangular entrance, with a lintel of wood or stone.

The first innovation was a longitudinal dividing wall, splitting the chamber in two, and affording greater space with less expenditure of building material and time in construction. Next, the chamber was elongated and the number of entrances increased, a procedure which gave rise, no doubt, to the square column; the next development, though neither the round column nor the pilaster appeared till after the Toltez invasion, at a much later period. Later, the buildings were greatly enlarged, split up into a number of parallel intercommunicating corridors, and a roof comb was added for decorative purposes. Finally, an inner shrine, or sanctuary, was built on, with stone benches, or altars, recesses, and sometimes narrow windows, though as a rule both light and air were admitted solely through the doors, in consequence of which the inner rooms must have been in a state of semi-darkness, even on the lightest days.

The vast majority of the private houses were almost certainly built of wood, thatched with palm leaves, the walls in some cases being covered with adobe. These have disappeared completely, incorporated in the layer of humus which now covers all Maya sites like a blanket. The better-class private houses were built of stone, to a height of about six feet from the ground. The roof was thatched and the walls covered with smooth hard stucco. These houses all stood upon small truncated pyramids, solidly constructed of rubble, blocks of stone, and loose mortar.

The primary object of the Maya architect of sacred buildings was, undoubtedly, not interior space but external magnificence and imposing display; in fact, a large and impressive building exhibiting a great expanse of brightly painted sculpture or stucco moulding, standing well up as a landmark above the city which surrounded it, and calculated to catch the eye and excite the imagination of everyone who beheld it. This is well exemplified by the vast and lofty temples on their massive substructures at Tzibanchè, where the rooms are so narrow, though long and lofty, that two persons cannot pass each other in them without turning sideways.

Again, it was a constant habit of the Maya to build out solid extensions from their temple, which, while they increased both the size and the height of the original structure, did not add an inch to its room space.

Sculpture.—The art of the Maya carver in stone was employed, so far as we know, exclusively in the service of the gods, fashioning their images, decorating their temples, and sculpturing the monoliths erected in their honor every five years, which last constituted the most important products of this art.

The stone employed varied with the locality: Andesite in Copan, sandstone and conglomerate in Quirigua, and limestone in Naranjo, Benque Viejo, and throughout Yucatan.

The artist must have been greatly handicapped in his work by the absence of any but stone tools, and though copper was introduced at a later date, it was far from plentiful and never appears to have superseded stone in the construction of the sculptor's tools.

In carving the stelæ greenstone chisels were chiefly used, and thousands of these have been found, of all sizes and in every stage of wear, especially in the neighborhood of Copan, where the most magnificent sculptures and the highest relief were achieved.

The salient characteristic of Maya sculpture is the fact that it is almost invariably in relief.

In the earliest specimens the relief was low, but as time went on the artist obtained a greater command over his material, the figures projected more and more prominently from the background, till at length they almost emerged from it and stood out in the round.

The Maya artist, in his knowledge of perspective, was probably more advanced than any contemporary throughout the world, and in purity of line is unexcelled possibly even at the present day. His presentation of the human figure in profile, and even in three-quarter view, leave little room for criticism. Perhaps the greatest fault which can be found with the Maya sculptor is his abhorrence of any vacant space, and the consequent introduction of such a wealth of detail that one sometimes loses the meaning of the design in the superabundance of decorative motifs which overlie it; in fact, "one cannot see the wood for the tree."

Originally, all sculpture was naturalistically colored, and it is possible that this coloration caused the principal figures to stand out so clearly from the too-elaborate background, that this criticism would no longer apply.

Maya art was, at all times, highly conventional, and the artist rarely escapes from the influence of religious symbolism, even in the fabrication of small objects. To what extent portraiture, as we understand it, had advanced it is difficult to say defintely, but the fact that strong emotions of various kinds are skilfully portrayed on many of the faces, and such personal idiosyncrasies as unilaterel facial paralysis are accurately recorded, would lead one to suppose that it had made considerable progress; moreover, one cannot avoid the conclusion that the life-sized human figures sculptured upon the monuments are actual presentments of contemporary priests and rulers.

Painting.—The Maya were extremely fond of color, and their censers, monoliths, sculpture, and temple walls were originally nearly all painted. Here, however, the colors were accessories, the work of the house painter, and all that survive to us of the works of the Maya pictorial artist are the codices, the wall frescoes, and designs on ceramic ware.

The codices contain highly conventionalized figures of deities, with intricate calculations as to the divisions of the year over which they presided. This material had to be crowded into as small a space as possible on the

Courtesy of Mr. F. Blom, Century of Progress Fair.

PLATE X.   UXMAL

A gateway into the quadrangle of the Monjas showing typical corbelled arch.

manuscript, and the correct identification of the gods by their dress and occupation, and accuracy in the intricate astrological calculations, were matters of far greater importance than mere artistic merit, in the eyes of the compiler. The codices were, in fact, primarily pictographs and arithmetical calculations rather than works of art. The colors used in them are red, black, blue, and green. The earliest dates from about 1000 A.D., and none go back to the Old Empire.

The frescoes are in very much the same category as the codices, and though on a much larger scale they also are rather pictographs than naturalistic works of art.

The human figures are highly conventionalized and loaded with a wealth of ornament and decoration, every detail of which had some special significance to the eyes of the initiated, and was meticulously portrayed. Few of these frescoes have survived in even moderately good preservation.

One at Santa Rita, in British Honduras, records the events which occurred during a certain time period, which, as the dates are in Maya glyphs and the figures are Mexican, must have been after the Toltec invasion of Yucatan.

A second fresco, at Tuluum, on the east coast of Yucatan, presents various avatars of the gods and belongs to an even later period than Santa Rita, for this city is known to have been occupied by the natives till well after the Spanish conquest.

The painter on pottery was not bound down by such

rigid conventionalism as handicapped the codex and fresco artists, and not being confined to purely religious subjects was permitted a far greater freedom of expression in depicting the human form. Men and women engaged in various occupations, animals, birds, fishes, and plants are all painted on pottery, the colors used being red, black, yellow, white, green, and blue. The purity of line in some of these little pictures is remarkable, and the artist, in some cases, even endeavors to give one the impression of motion in the human fingers and to convey an effect of perspective without the aid of shading.

The finest pieces are very rare and found, unfortunately, for the most part in fragments, but a good deal of somewhat inferior work, in which the artist was rather slovenly, both in design and technic, as if he aimed rather at mass production than at quality, is fairly common and belongs probably to a late period.

Pottery.—With the exception possibly of Peru, the Maya era produced the most beautiful pottery found anywhere in ancient America.

The potter's wheel was unknown in the Western Hemisphere before the arrival of Europeans, which led to a certain individuality in even the commonest domestic pieces turned out by each potter.

Three methods of fabricating pottery were commonly employed. The simplest consisted in modelling, or shaping a vessel from a lump of clay, with the fingers. Larger pots were built up by coiling a flat ribbon of plastic clay spirally around the vessel till the desired side was reached, the junctions of the spirals being smoothed off with a flat, spoon-shaped implement of pottery or wood. Lastly, vessels, usually the smaller ones, were made in clay moulds. Sometimes the vessel was moulded in two portions, subsequently joined together, and this was more frequently done if one side of it was covered with elaborate relief ornament.

Various methods of decoration were employed. Sometimes a design was incised upon the vessel while the clay was still moist and plastic, or again it might be stamped on by means of a mould. In a second process the design was engraved upon the hard surface of the vessel after it had been baked, and lastly, and this process was employed almost exclusively in the fabrication of large censers, the decoration was effected in the form of high relief appliquè figures, upon the outer surface of the vessel, before it was baked. In conjunction with, or independently of, these methods, the ware was painted in various colors, the commonest being red, yellow, black, and green, either directly upon its surface or upon a thin slip or wash of clay previously applied all over it.

The pottery was probably fired under glowing charcoal, as this was the method in vogue amongst the Maya at the time of the Conquest, and it is probable that had the kiln method even been discovered it would have persisted, at any rate, in some localities.

The paste used varied a good deal according to the

use to which the vessel was to be put. In domestic utensils it was coarse and contained a considerable proportion of powdered stone, shell, or gourd, and was not always well fired. In the decorated ware, however, it was of a porcelain-like fineness. It varied a good deal in color through various shades of cream, yellow, red, brown, and black.

Certain objects, as painted ware and moulded figurines, appear to have been manufactured only in special localities and to have been very widely distributed from these centres over the entire Maya area, and even in some cases outside this.

This fact should, when Maya ceramics have been more carefully investigated, afford us considerable knowledge of the trade routes of both the Old and New Empire. Considerable differences exist in style and technic between the wares of the early, the middle, and the late periods, and the recent discovery of a refuse cave at Pusilhà has shown the possibility of stylistic dating, held out by a more intensive study of these differences.

Minor Arts. Spinning and Weaving.—Wool was, of course, unknown to the Maya, but very beautiful fabrics were woven from cotton, and coarse-grade material from the fibre of the *Agave americana* and species of cactus. A few pieces of coarse cotton cloth, found by Mr. Franz Blom in a cave in Mexico, are all that have as yet been found of Maya textiles of the Old Empire, and only a few fragments, found buried in the mud at the bottom of the cenote at Chichen-Itza, have survived from the New Empire. We know, however, from the evidence of the monuments and the codices, that the designs were very beautiful and intricate, sometimes of diamond patterned openwork, and usually embroidered in a great variety of devices, into which men, gods, animals, birds, fishes, flowers, and geometrical figures were all introduced. They were dyed in a variety of colors, of which red, yellow, and blue were most frequently employed, obtained from native cochineal, fustic, and indigo. Gorgeous feathers of the humming bird, parrot, quetzal, and macaw were also cleverly woven into their fabrics.

Spinning was practised by women of all classes, and the objects most frequently met with around every ancient Maya site to-day are the circular spindle whorls of clay or stone.

Weaving was done on a common hand loom, the strips of cloth, which rarely exceeded fifteen inches in breadth, being subsequently sewn together.

Basketry.—The Maya probably never arrived at the perfection in this art reached by some of their American contemporaries. Huge coarse earthenware pots seem to have been used for storing dry food stuffs, and coarse-fibred henequen bags for carrying purposes, the two chief uses of basketry amongst primitive people. Basket work was, however, used to a limited extent, for the backs of their shields were of this material, and some of the large receptacles for corn were undoubtedly coarsely woven from whole withies and liana, as were also, on occasion, the doors and upper parts of the walls of their houses.

Wood Carving.—The few specimens which have come down to us from the Old Empire indicate that, in beauty and complexity of design, and in the most fault-less technic of their execution, they have seldom been excelled by the wood carvers of any age. The carving is always done in low-relief panels on beams or lintels. The wood used is invariably sapodillo, which, if not exposed to the weather and the incursions of white ants, will last almost indefintely and has survived at Tikal and Tzibanchè for fifteen centuries.

The monoliths erected every five years were, prob-ably, before the introduction of stone, made of wood, as the technic of the wood carver has been transmitted to the earliest stone monuments.

Images of the gods were also carved in wood, in the round, and were greatly prized but none of these have come down to us. A few small carved wooden objects have been found preserved in the mud of the cenote, notably spear throwers, which show the same perfection in technic as is displayed in the beams and lintels.

Metal Working.—With two doubtful exceptions, the only metal found in the cities of the Old Empire was a small quantity of mercury beneath a stela at Copan, and even in this case it is probable that the metal was produced by the contact of cinnabar with some reducing agent, over a period of fifteen centuries. The two exceptions are a small gold head, reputed to have been found in the city of Palenque, and a gold whistle and epaulette-like object, said to have come from a site near Tikal.

It is rather curious that gold ornaments were not, apparently, used to any extent by the Old Empire Maya, for the metal is found, in the form of nuggets of considerable size, near several of their ancient sites, and one would imagine that the beauty of the metal and the facility in working it would have appealed to them.

Copper and bronze objects were common during the New Empire, though the admixture of tin with the copper was probably accidental. Copper axe heads and chisels are found, but they are not common, and never, probably, superseded stone to any great extent, except in the fabrication of rings, bells, ear plugs, gorgets, and other objects of personal adornment.

Gold ornaments occur in considerable numbers in the cenote at Chichen-Itza, and carved wooden objects covered with a thin foil of gold have also been found.

The gold figurines from the same source were almost certainly imported from Costa Rica as trade pieces. The Maya were indeed never great workers in metals, stone being always their favorite medium, and most of the gold and copper ornaments found in the Maya area were imported from the south or from Mexico.

Flint and Obsidian Working and Jade Carving.— The flint and obsidian ornaments and weapons produced by the Maya were unsurpassed in technic by any found throughout the world, except perhaps in Egypt and Denmark.

Spearheads, javelin blades, knives, and arrowheads were manufactured both by percussion and by pressure, but perhaps the greatest command over these intractable materials was shown in the curious eccentrically shaped objects, the manufacture of which was confined to the Maya area. These assume the forms of crosses, crescents, rings, and various fantastic shapes. Some represent animals, rabbits, snakes, or birds, and some are chipped into human form.

They vary in size from an inch or two to a couple of feet in length. Their function is not known, but they are usually found associated with burials, and, like the small clay figurines, were probably ceremonial cinerary objects.

Jade ornaments were regarded by the Maya as their most valuable possessions, and at working this intractable material, with stone tools alone, they were extraordinarily clever. Beads, ear plugs, masks, and gorgets were the objects most frequently manufactured. The flat plaques, used as gorgets, were sculptured with anthropomorphic figures, chiefly those of gods. These were probably blocked out in the rough with stone chisels and then smoothed and finished by friction with fine sand and water.

The jade used appears to have been confined solely to water-worn pebbles, found in the beds of streams, as, during the early Old Empire, large ornaments of jade were produced, during the late Old Empire smaller objects, and during the New Empire, when the supply seems to have become practically exhausted, only very small articles, such as beads and studs.

Jade has never been found in its natural state in the Maya area, and it seems almost certain, from its rarity and the extravagant value which both they and the Mexicans placed upon it, that their only sources of supply were the beds of rivers.

CHAPTER V

RELIGION
(J. E. T.)

Sources of our information as to the ancient Maya religion. Historical sources. Images of the gods in stone and pottery. The codices. Present-day survivals of the ancient religion. The earth gods and the lords of the forests. Prayer to the lord of the hills and valleys. The Chacs of Yucatan. Itzamna, the sky god, and his attributes. Kinich Ahau, the sun god, and his hieroglyph. The worship of the morning star. Ah Puch, the ruler of the underworld. The Maya conception of hell and heaven. Extensive pantheon introduced later. The various grades of priests and their functions. Vestal virgins. Human sacrifice during the Old Empire. Method of sacrificing victims by excising the heart while still alive, by shooting to death with arrows, and by drowning in the cenote at Chichen-Itza. Other sacrifices to the gods. Loss of the ancient Maya idols. The cult of
Kukulcan, or the Feathered Serpent.

OUR information on Maya religion is derived from several sources. The first of these is represented by the accounts contained in sixteenth-century Spanish documents. Among the early writers Bishop Landa alone has left a fairly full description of Maya deities and religious festivals. As the sections of his book dealing with native customs and beliefs were based either on the information supplied by a highly intelligent Maya, Gaspar Xiu, or were actually written by this man after his conversion to Christianity, the information is, although meagre, of great importance for a study of Maya religion. Villagutierre and Cogolludo also lift the curtain somewhat on this subject, although the latter's information was borrowed from an earlier though less known writer—Aguilar. These writers were acquainted with Maya religion as practised in Yucatan. For Guatemala we are indebted to a Spanish friar, Jimenez, who, speaking Quiche perfectly, reduced a number of the old Maya-Quiche legends and stories of the gods to writing, and further translated them into Spanish, in a history he wrote of Guatemala and Chiapas. An outline of these legends is given in Chapter VI.

In addition to the information obtained from these historical sources, a light has been shed on Maya religion by a study of the portraits of Maya gods carved in stone on the stelæ and temples, and painted on pottery, and the leaves of the three surviving Maya manuscripts. The difficulty has been to co-ordinate the descriptions and attributes of the separate deities unaccompanied by illustrations, which the early post-conquest writers have left us, with the carvings and paintings of gods unaccompanied by descriptions.

There is a further, and as yet almost untouched, source of information on Maya religion. At the present time most of the Maya peoples, although nominal Christians, retain many of the beliefs and customs of their pagan ancestors. Sometimes these beliefs have been adulterated by Christian influences, but in many cases the chaff can be separated from the wheat, leaving a mass of purely Maya religion.

Most discussions of Maya religion have entirely omitted this modern ethnological source, and attempted

to elucidate Maya religious concepts on the basis of the
first two sources only. In this chapter the religious beliefs of the Mayas will be approached mainly from the
ethnological side, while the description of the actual
ceremonies will be based on the written sources, and to
a less extent on such information as the manuscripts
and monuments yield to us.

Maya civilization, like that of the peoples of Mexico, was based on agriculture. Without agriculture, and
in particular the annual sowing and harvesting of the
maize crop, Maya civilization would have speedily and
inevitably collapsed. Consequently Maya religion centred around the propitiation and worship of the personified powers of nature.

Far and away the most important Maya deities were
those that personified the earth. These earth gods were
considered to be innumerable, but there were four of
outstanding importance, and of these one was chief,
superior to the other three, and ruler of all the rank
and file of earth gods. The four principal personifications of the soil were associated with the four world
directions, east, north, west, and south. They were also
associated with the four world colors, yellow, red,
white, and black. Around these gods Maya daily life
and daily religion revolved. Among most Maya tribes
they were known under names which can be translated
as "Mountain-valley." They were the surface of the
earth and consequently the mountains and valleys. In
Yucatan they were, and are to this day, for they are

PLATE XI.   MAYA GODS FROM THE DRESDEN CODEX

1-3. The long-nosed earth and rain god. 4. The sky god. 5. The sun god. 6. God C, the monkey-faced god. 7. The maize spirit. 8. The death god. 9. The goddess of suicides. 10. The god of war.

still worshipped, accorded the title of Yumil Kaxob, "Lords of the forests." Yucatan is for the most part level country, and for this reason a title such as "Mountain-valley" would be meaningless, but on the other hand the whole country is covered with forest, and therefore the lords of the forest are lords of all the country. They are also known as "The mighty ones," "The captains who go before," and in Guatemala as "Mamob," "The old ones," or as "The builders."

As personifications of the soil they are primarily patrons of agriculture, and to them are addressed prayers for successful crops when the forest is felled to make the fields, and when the seed is sown. None of the prayers that were offered up to them before the coming of the Spaniards have survived, nevertheless the prayers addressed to them by the conservative Maya of to-day probably differ but slightly from those that have been poured forth season after season without a break for over two thousand years.

Below is given a typical modern prayer addressed to Huitz-Hok, which means just "Mountain-valley." This prayer was obtained by the writer from a small Maya village in the south of British Honduras, and is the one used before cutting down the forest to prepare the field for sowing. Its charm lies in its simplicity, apologizing to the Huitz-Hok for the disfigurement that will be caused to the earth god's face by cutting down the forest and digging the ground, and at the same time interceding for a good crop.

"O God, my mother, my father, Huitz-Hok, Lord Hills and Valleys, Che, Lord Forest, be patient with me for I am about to do as my fathers have ever done. Now I make my offering (of copal) to you that you may know that I am about to trouble your very soul, but suffer it, I pray you. I am about to dirty you—to destroy your beauty—I am going to work you that I may obtain my daily bread. I pray you suffer no animal to attack me, nor snake to bite me. Permit not the scorpion or wasp to sting me. Bid the trees that they fall not upon me, and suffer not the axe or knife to cut me, for with all my heart I am about to work you."

The mountain-valley gods are also known as "Mam," which means grandfather. The earth is old. It has been here since the beginning, and the mountain-valley gods, too, are old in wisdom and years. They are our grandfathers, and look after their grandchildren. They send the crops. They look after the animals in the forest and allow their grandchildren to hunt them. They are benevolent and not exacting, for all they ask is that they be prayed to, and offered copal incense.

They are also gods of rain and thunder and lightning. They send the rains to nourish the crops, and when, as sometimes happens, they are angry, they hurl their thunderbolts from the mountain tops. Possibly they have taken over the sending of rain from other gods, whose special function this was, and whose identity has now been merged in that of the earth gods. As patrons of rain the earth gods, or the gods who have been merged into them, are known in Yucatan as Chacs. Each Chac has a small calabash of water, a bag which holds the winds, and a drum. They take the calabash of water and sprinkle a little of its contents down on the world, and the rain descends on the earth. To send a wind they open the bag slightly and let a little of the wind escape. When they wish to stop the wind blowing they force it back into the bag. The thunder they cause by beating their drum.

A long-nosed god, who is frequently depicted in the codices and on the monuments, is probably Chac. He is often shown carrying an axe. (Plates XI, 1–3; XII, 1 and 2.) This is the symbol of thunder, for the Maya believes that damage done by lightning is caused by the Chacs striking with their axes. In fact, stone axes are called by the modern Maya Chac's axes, and are believed to have been hurled down to earth by the Chacs. Furthermore, this long-nosed god is often shown with a maize plant growing out of his head, a symbol of his patronage of agriculture. Scenes in the codices also show the long-nosed god actually sowing maize. The Chac associated with the south is unlucky and a death-dealer. He is depicted with a long nose too, but the body of a skeleton. He is probably thus shown because he rules the corner of the world, whence come the hot scorching winds that dry up the young crops, and cause famine. However, on the whole the earth gods are distinctly benevolent. They are the gods of a simple agricultural people. They are the gods of

Courtesy of the Field Museum.

PLATE XII. MAYA GODS FROM THE MONUMENTS

1–2. The long-nosed earth and rain god. 3. The moon deity. 4. The sun god. 5. God C, the monkey-faced god. 6. The maize spirit. 7. The death god.

the layman as opposed to the more complex and esoteric concepts of an exclusive priesthood steeped in astrology. With these earth deities with their numerous titles and their functions, original or borrowed, we are face to face with the fundamentals of Maya religion. They are the basic gods, to whom the rank and file clung, and still cling, despite persecution and attempts to force other gods upon them. The Maya, who lives so close to the soil, is attached with a passionate devotion to these friendly patrons of his fields. For these gods, in return for simple prayers and humble offerings of copal incense, realize the peasant's greatest desire by sending a bountiful harvest. For this reason they are the most important of the Maya gods.

As opposed to the earth deities there were gods associated with the sky. The chief of these was Itzamna, who was the ruler of the sky. He was credited with the introduction of writing, and was said to have been the son of the creator god, Hunab Kuh, the first god. Itzamna was also worshipped under the name of Yaxkokamut. He can probably be identified with a familiar deity in the codices and on the monuments, who is invariably shown with a prominent Roman nose, and a mouth which is either toothless or possesses only the stump of one tooth. (Plate XI, 4.)

In addition to the sky god there was a sun god, who was known in Yucatan as Kinich Ahau, "Lord of the Sun." Among a number of the Maya tribes the sun would appear to have had a close connection with the jaguar. In fact, among certain of the Maya tribes of the Highlands or Guatemala one of his titles was the Jaguar. The sun is the hero of a series of legends, that recount his life and adventures on earth before he ascended to the sky to take up his duties as the sun. Fragments of these legends are to be found in the "Popol Vuh," a synopsis of which is given in Chapter VI. The sun can be recognized with certainty on the monuments and in the codices. He is nearly always shown as bearded, and usually carries either in his head-dress or in the ornament pendant from his ear-plug the hieroglyph for a day, an oval with a small nick in each corner enclosed in a cartouche. (Plates XI, 5, and XII, 4.)

The moon would appear to have been feminine, and legend has it that she was the wife of the sun. She used to be as bright as the sun, as a result there was no darkness on earth, and the people complained that they could not get any sleep. To remedy that the sun plucked out one of his spouse's eyes, and since then the moon has not shone with the same brilliance.

None of these sky deities are of particular importance compared to the earth gods. However, there was one god connected with the sky who was of paramount importance. This was the god of the planet Venus, particularly in his manifestation as morning star. In Yucatan he was known as Ah Noh Ich, "Lord big eye." The importance of the morning star is to be found in the fact that the cycle of the planet Venus played a very important part in Maya calendarical calculations.

(See Chapter VIII.) He was the god of the astronomers, who were at the same time the priests. Calculations revolved around his reappearance as morning star, and he was intimately connected with the fifty-two-year cycle, with the end of which it was believed, sooner or later, would coincide the end of the world. There seems no reason to doubt that the priesthood deliberately foisted the worship of Venus on the Maya layman, attempting to supplant the old earth gods with this new religion. The Maya peasants were taught that the morning star was the real patron of agriculture and hunting, and prayers for a successful hunt or for good crops must be addressed to him. Apparently a compromise was eventually reached, either unofficially by the rank and file, or with the consent of the priests, and the morning star was recognized as patron of agriculture, hunting and fishing, but was conceded to have delegated his powers to the earth gods, the "Mountain-valleys."

Venus as Morning star seems to have been symbolized by a monster, who was a cross between a dragon and a snake, and whose body was covered with feathers of the quetzal bird instead of the usual scales of the snake. This concept would appear to be late, and probably was adopted only toward the end of the so-called "Old Empire," and then probably only by the priesthood, with any enthusiasm.

As there were deities associated with the earth and others that ruled in the sky, so there were gods connected with the other sphere recognized by the Maya —the underworld. The ruler of the Maya underworld was called Ah Puch or Hun Ahau. He is depicted as a skeleton, or with a human body covered with the stains of decomposition. (Plate XI, 8.) He is also usually shown wearing a collar of bells. The Mayas believed in a future existence after this life. The rank and file and, according to the early Spanish friars, those that had led evil lives went after death to Metnal. Metnal was a dank, gloomy, cold spot beneath the earth, where those dead who belonged to the divisions enumerated above continued to live. Here under Ah Puch's rule they suffered an existence of gloomy ennui, relieved only by the periodic spells of intense cold. There was, however, no torture, such as is promised the evil-doers of our civilization by the diminishing bands of Fundamentalists. Those who had committed suicide went to a special abode, which was a paradise in every sense of the word. Judging from Mexican analogues this abode was ruled over by the Chacs or earth gods. The description of this paradise as a place where wonderful fruits and vegetables are found in profusion strengthens the supposition that it was, indeed, ruled over by the patrons of agriculture. The third land of the dead was, again according to the Spanish friars, who tended to inject Christianity into the pagan beliefs they recorded, reserved for those who had led good lives upon earth. However, in all probability, this heaven, which was situated in the sky, was the residence after death of those who had held high rank while on earth—the warriors, priests, those who had been sacrificed, and women who had died in childbirth. This conjecture is based on the known beliefs of the Aztecs and other Mexican peoples whose religious beliefs were closely allied to those of the Mayas.

In later times at least the Mayas believed in a host of relatively unimportant deities who were patrons of some special occupation or personifications of elements. Such were the gods of war, of fire, and the spirits of maize and cacao. The last was by extension also patron of merchants and trade in general for the reason that cacao beans served as the medium of exchange.

Large numbers of priests were required to minister to so many gods, and to perform the numerous ceremonies considered necessary by such an intensely religious people as the Maya. The chief priest was known as the Ah Kin Mai, and he was usually the second son of the chief. He was called on to officiate only at very special functions, his duties for the most part consisting of the teaching of the young priests. These he taught how to read and write hieroglyphs, how to manipulate the calendar, and how to read the future. Below Ah Kin Mai were the regular priests, whose chief duty was to officiate at sacrifices, and interpret the wishes of the gods to their followers. They were known as the Chilans. The Nacons were special priests, whose sole duty was to tear out the hearts of sacrificial victims. They wore their hair long and matted with the blood of the victims they had sacrificed, and were clad in long white cotton dresses that reached to the ground. Below them were a grade of lay priests, called Chacs, whose chief duty was to hold down the arms and legs of the sacrificial victims. Four were elected by each town, and held office for the space of one year, after which they were replaced by four other elders chosen from the community. In addition to the priests there were groups of virgins, who lived in convents under the guardianship of a mother superior. They were responsible for sweeping the temples and temple courts, and were especially charged with keeping the sacred fire alight. The ranks of the vestal virgins were recruited voluntarily, and all were free to leave whenever they chose. These young women were of high rank, and after a few years' service left to marry warriors or members of the nobility.

It has been suggested that the Mayas at the time when the cities of the so-called Old Empire were at their bloom did not practise human sacrifice. However, evidence is accumulating that such was not the case. At the city of Piedras Negras there is a stela, at the base of which is carved a victim stretched across a sacrificial block with a deep gash across his breast, from which spurts a stream of blood. Furthermore at a number of Maya cities of the early period votive caches have been discovered under altars or the floors of temples, which contained decapitated heads placed in bowls. Finally a magnificent altar at Tikal is carved with a design of heads placed in bowls. It is true that these heads have the features of the long-nosed god, but the Central American Indians believed that a victim assumed the divinity of the god to whom he was sacrificed, and that is probably the reason why the heads in the bowls on the altar at Tikal have divine features. Nevertheless human sacrifice was never as frequent as among the Aztecs, where on one occasion, it is said, 70,000 victims were sacrificed at the dedication of a temple.

Prisoners of war usually supplied the victims for sacrifice. However, in times of great stress, when no prisoners were available a community would subscribe to buy slaves to sacrifice, and very devout men would even offer their own children. The victims were kept in small wooden cages until they were required. Before being sacrificed the victim was stripped of his clothing and painted with a blue unguent, blue being the sacrificial color. He was led up the steps of the pyramid to the foot of the temple perched on its summit. In front of the temple was a small block of limestone with a convex top, not unlike the mile stones to be found along English roads. The wretched man was placed over this stone, so that the convex top of the stone fitted into the small of his back. Two of the Chacs at his head held his hands firmly, while the other two each held a foot. In this position he was helpless, with his breast exposed to receive the sacrificial knife. The officiating priest, cutting open his chest with a special knife of obsidian or flint, mounted with a richly decorated handle, plunged

PLATE XIII.   A HUMAN SACRIFICE

The victim is stretched out on an altar made of the coiled body of a feathered serpent. The chief priest stands above, knife in hand, ready to remove the victim's heart. The drawing was made by Mrs. A. Morris from a damaged fresco.

his hand into the wound, and tore out the wretch's heart almost before it had ceased to palpitate. The heart he placed on an earthen dish and offered up to the sun, after which he smeared the idol's face with it. The lifeless carcass was hurled down the steep sides of the pyramid to the waiting crowd beneath. Priests and warriors crowded round to snatch a part of the body, which now partook of the divinity to which it had been sacrificed. The flesh was taken home and eaten in a kind of communion service, thereby endowing him who consumed it with divine grace. Special portions such as the hands and feet were reserved for the officiating priest. This ceremonial eating of the victim was not cannibalism in the general meaning of that word, as the flesh was not eaten for its savor, but for the grace with which it endowed the eater. Sometimes the skin was reserved, and the priest, donning it, took part in a special ceremonial dance, and continued to wear it for several days. If the victim had been a prisoner of war, his captor was awarded the jawbone, and wore this as a proof of his prowess.

Another form of human sacrifice was occasionally practised. In this case the prisoner, painted in the sacrificial blue, and with a white circle marked over his heart, was tied to a post in the square in front of the chief pyramid. The men of the community assembled with their bows and arrows, and on the signal being given by the priest, began to revolve slowly round the victim in a dancing circle, keeping time to the music of the drums, flutes, and tortoise carapaces. Gradually the rhythm of the music changed, growing faster and faster. Then, on a signal from the priest, each man as he came opposite raised his bow, and shot an arrow into the circle marked on the victim's breast, till the wretch expired, transfixed by a multitude of arrows.

Men and even young girls were hurled into deep pools of water in an attempt to propitiate the rain gods. A number of years ago the sacred pool at Chichen-Itza was partially dragged, and among the objects brought to the surface were gold and jade ornaments, and the bones of young women. If the victim, after being hurled into this pool from a great height, was found to be still alive at mid-day, he or she was pulled out, and accorded great honor. The great leader Kukulcan was said to have risen to his high rank in this manner after surviving the requisite time in the well at Chichen-Itza. (See Chapter III.)

Besides human beings all manner of animals, birds and fruits were offered to the gods. Dogs in particular were very frequently sacrificed. These were specially bred for eating, and were considered a great luxury, and for that reason very pleasing to the gods. Deer and turkeys were also offered in large quantities, as well as all manner of dishes made of maize and squash seeds. Each offered according to his wealth and rank. Whereas a person of rank would offer jade ornaments, his most prized possession, the poor man would content himself with an offering of maize, or cacao. All sacrifices were invariably accompanied by the burning of copal incense, or the gum of the white acacia.

Practically none of the large idols to which these sacrifices were made have survived to the present time. The great majority of those in the temples of Yucatan at the time of the arrival of the Spaniards suffered destruction at the hands of fanatical friars and priests, and the rest were hidden away to await the better times that never came. Most of them were, we are told, made of wood, and these would not long withstand the damp climate of Central America. However, many of the smaller idols of pottery and stone have survived, and many figures of gods that may have been used solely for adornment have been excavated in the cities of Honduras and Yucatan. In many cases these were used as decorative elements on the façades of temples, stone sculpture in the round being somewhat rare. A phallic cult existed in Yucatan in late times, but this may well have been the result of Mexican influence.

Chichen-Itza was the centre of the cult of a mysterious god, Kukulcan, whose name is said to mean "feathered serpent," and who was worshipped in the guise of a rattlesnake with a body whose scales were replaced by the feathers of the sacred quetzal bird (Plate XIII). He was the Maya counterpart of the Mexican deity Quetzalcoatl, whose name, too, means "Quetzal bird-serpent." He, too, is of almost as mysterious nature as Kukulcan. Apparently there were two Kukulcans—one a god, and the other a religious and civil leader who bore the same name. The histories of the two are inextricably mixed. However, as suggested above, the feathered serpent was probably the guise under which the planet Venus was worshipped, at least in early times. Nevertheless, Quetzalcoatl, or Kukulcan, was more than a god of the morning star. In Mexico he was also a wind god, a god of the air, and possibly something approaching a chief deity to the Toltecs. In Guatemala under the name of Gucamatz, which also means "feathered serpent," he was worshipped as one of the four creator gods. Again it is impossible to say whether such belief arose as a result of Mexican contacts. It would seem safer frankly to shirk the problem of trying to elucidate what the feathered serpent meant to the Maya until such time as more has been learned about Maya religion. It is noteworthy that there is no trace, as far as is at present known, of any worship of such a deity among the present-day Mayas, either of the peninsula of Yucatan or of the highlands of Guatemala. This would suggest that such a cult did not form a part of native Maya religion, but was forced on the soil-loving Mayas by outside influences, possibly the result of invasion, such as we know occurred in Yucatan.

Maya religion was intimately bound up with the calendar. The nights and the days were under the patronage of different gods, and so too were the different periods into which the calendar was divided. We might hazard the guess that the figures carved on many of the stelæ represent the gods who ruled over the special day, or period, which the stela was erected to commemorate. However, in the end all is subordinate to the great god of the Maya, the land and its produce. The complex calendar existed to tell him the favorable moment to sow or harvest his crops, the gods, who directly or indirectly affected his harvests, he has created to guard and benefit his maize crop, the alpha and omega of Maya religion.

CHAPTER VI

RELIGIOUS CEREMONIES AND TRADITIONS
(J. E. T.)

Reputed visit of St. Thomas to the New World. Baptism amongst the Maya, its ritual and significance. Baptism actually a ceremony signifying that children, both male and female, had reached puberty. Confession amongst the Maya. Their reluctance to public confession. Sins of intent not confessed. Offerings to the gods of blood of various parts of the body. The Maya new year. Elaborate ceremonies and long fasts associated with it. Renewal of all household utensils. Kindling the sacred fires in the temples. Drunkenness not common amongst the Maya. Forecasting the weather for the year. Feasts held by the hunters, fishermen, and bee-keepers. Annual feast in honor of the god Kukulcan was a national ceremony amongst the Maya. Fashioning the new wooden idols and the feast connected with this ceremony. The feast of the Chacs. The feasts of the Cacao planters and of the warriors. The *Popol Vuh*, sacred book of the Quichè. Its creation legends. Various experiments by the creator gods in producing a satisfactory race of men, till eventually men as they are to-day were created. Legends of the adventures of the divine brothers Hunapu and Xbalanque, also of the brothers Hunhunahpu and Vukub Hunahpu amongst the people of the Underworld.

THE Mayas performed a number of ceremonies that bore a superficial resemblance to some of the rites of the Catholic church. This similarity gave rise to a belief among some of the Spaniards that Saint Thomas had preached the gospel in the new world. However, there is no reason at all to credit such a theory.

The Mayas practised a form of baptism, which particularly seemed to the early frairs to prove their contention. Furthermore, the Maya word used to denote this ceremony meant "rebirth." However, the children were baptized when about twelve years old, and not soon after birth as among Christians. The baptism was the occasion for a feast for the whole community. The father of a child to be baptized gave notice to the priest, and a lucky day was picked, and any other member of the community who had children of an age fit for baptism was invited. For the three days that preceded the ceremony the parents fasted and remained continent. On the day of the feast all assembled in the court of the house of the parent who was responsible for the feast. The floor had previously been swept clean, and strewn with leaves, and there the children were gathered together, the boys in one group under an old man, who served as a kind of godfather, the girls apart in another group under the tutelage of an old woman.

The courtyard was next purified. This was the task of the four Chacs, who, as pointed out in the previous chapter, were junior lay priests. At each corner of the patio was placed a low stool, on which the Chacs sat. Ropes were stretched from each corner, forming a kind of corral, inside which were the children. The priest sat on another small stool in the centre. Each child came up to him in turn, and receiving from him a little ground maize and copal incense, took it, and threw it into a brazier. When all the children had done this, the brazier, the ropes that had been used to form the corral, and a little of the balche wine were given to a man to take away. The man had to carry the material out of

the town without looking at it, and throw it away in
some unfrequented spot. The idea seems to have been
that the evil in the children passed into the ground
maize and incense they held in their hands, and by
throwing these away, their inherent evil was at the
same time disposed of. A similar ceremony is still in
use among the modern Mayas of British Honduras to
cure sickness.

Leaves of the wild fig tree were now substituted for
those on the floor of the patio, and the priest dressed in
his plumed vestments. Next the Chacs approached the
children, and tied white cloths round their heads, bid-
ding those that had committed some serious offence to
confess it, and separate themselves from the rest of the
children. The priest then blessed the children, and
sprinkled them with water with a short, finely carved
stick from which hung the tails of rattlesnakes. When
this was concluded the father who was giving the feast
took a special bone from the priest, and gave each child
nine sharp taps on the forehead with it. Then dipping
the bone in an unguent made of certain flowers, ground
cacao, and water, which had been collected from hol-
lows in tree trunks, he rubbed it on the faces and between the fingers and toes of the children. The white
cloths on their heads were next removed, and the priest,
taking a stone knife, cut the cord which held suspended
a special stone on the forehead. This stone they had
worn since they were babies and its removal signified
that they were now to be accepted as men. The boys

were then made to smell a special bouquet of flowers, and were given tobacco to smoke. Subsequently they were given special dishes of food, which their parents had brought them. The ceremony was now concluded, save that the mothers removed the shell which each girl had worn from childhood in front of her sexual organs. After the ceremony she was accepted as a woman, and free to marry. In the evening a big feast was held by the parents to mark the conclusion of these puberty ceremonies.

The Mayas, too, practised a form of confession, which also intrigued their early Christian instructors. However, the Mayas, ever a canny race, usually waited till an illness overtook them, before confessing. In fact, even then, they were often loath to confess, and had to be pressed by their relatives before they would send for a priest. The reason for this reluctance is probably to be found in the fact that sins were confessed in public, and Bishop Landa tells us that often, after a man had recovered, there were conjugal recriminations resulting from what the man had confessed during his illness. If there was no priest available the confession could be made to one's parents, or a man could confess to his wife or *vice versa*.

Robbery, homicide, fornication, and false testimony were the sins most commonly confessed, but, strangely enough, sins of intent were not confessed. It was believed that after confession the sick person stood a much better chance of recovery.

Before most important ceremonies the Mayas fasted, abstaining from salt, chili pepper, and on occasions from meat. The fasting was invariably accompanied by abstention from sexual intercourse. Priests, naturally, fasted more frequently than the laymen. Indeed, the fasts of leaders of the community might even last as long as three years.

A frequent form of sacrifice took the form of offering one's own blood. The men used to cut their ears, tongues, lower lips, cheeks, or other parts of their bodies, and pass straws through them. These straws with the human blood adhering were then offered in sacrifice to the gods. A very fine stone door lintel from the ruins of Yaxchilan, now in the British Museum, shows this form of sacrifice. (Plate V.) A seated individual, richly garbed, is shown passing a cord across the surface of his tongue. Into the cord at intervals are set thorns. These thorns, covered with the blood of the man's tongue, were deposited in a basket at the man's feet, and, presumably, subsequently offered to some deity.

The Maya new year, which fell at the beginning of the month Pop, was ushered in with elaborate ceremonies. Each year in turn was associated with one of the four chief earth gods, and correspondingly with the color and world direction with which that god was associated. Owing to the structure of the calendar only four day-signs could occupy the day 1 Pop. These were, at the time of the Spanish Conquest, Kan, Muluc, Ix, and Cauac. Apparently at some time during the so-called New Empire there had been a one-day shift, as during the ninth cycle, the days associated with 1 Pop had been Akbal, Lamat, Ben, and Eznab.

The years that commenced with a day Kan or a day Muluc were considered to be lucky, but the opposite was believed of years that commenced with the days Ix or Cauac. Droughts and failure of the crops were expected, as well as different diseases. Accordingly the ceremonies in connection with these years were particularly elaborate.

Fasting for the new year feast began some time before the actual date. In fact, the more devout actually started to fast as long as three months before the close of the year. The last five days of the old year were considered to be particularly unlucky. They were known as the nameless days, and during their passage no unnecessary work was undertaken. Neither men nor women combed their hair, nor washed themselves, and this must have been a real sacrifice for the Mayas, who were so fond of bathing. The people stayed indoors as much as possible, only going out to pray and make offerings in the temples.

On new year's day the houses were cleaned out, and all the household possessions, such as plates, beds, mats, etc., were renewed. The old possessions were taken outside the town and thrown away. The object being, apparently, to cast out the evil, as in the puberty ceremony described above. All the men of the community

PLATE XIV. LATE MAYA IDOL POSSIBLY DATING FROM
AFTER THE CONQUEST

From Tuluum.

flocked to the main temple, where the Chacs for the coming year were chosen from among the elders. At the temples, too, all the utensils had been renewed, and quantities of new copal incense laid out for the worshippers.

When all the men were assembled, for the women were not admitted to the different services in the temples, the ceremonies commenced. The men had exchanged the black paint they used while fasting, for red, and with their faces thus painted, and wearing their new garments, they witnessed the kindling of the sacred fire. Previously the temple fires had been extinguished, and now they were relit by the Chacs. The flame was obtained by twirling a stick of hard wood within a depression in a piece of soft wood. The friction engendered sufficient heat to kindle the dry powder that resulted. All the men of the congregation in turn approached, and offered incense, which they were given by the priest. The ceremony concluded with the drinking of large quantities of balche wine, and a general feast.

It must not be supposed that the Mayas were a very drunken race. The drinking of liquor was almost entirely ceremonial. It was part of the religious service, and only the old men were allowed to drink on other occasions; drunkenness on a non-ceremonial occasion being a very serious offence, severely punished.

During the month of Pop the priests were engaged in making their prognostications for the coming year.

It would appear that they foretold the weather for the rest of the year, according to the weather during the month of Pop, each day of Pop having power over the corresponding month in the year. That is if 5 Pop, which was the sixth day of the month, for example, was wet, that meant the sixth month of the year, Xul, would be wet. These prophecies were issued to the public, who, being farmers, were eagerly awaiting them, early in the month Uo. Other prophecies were read out of the sacred books by the priests, and the ceremony closed with a special dance known as the dance of the month Uo.

In the month Zip there was a special feast made by the hunters to the gods of the chase. The feast was held in the house of one of the principals, and as it did not take place in a temple, the women were allowed to be present. The principal feature was a dance, in which all the hunters took part, dancing round with the skull of a deer in one hand, and in the other an arrow. Both objects were painted the sacred blue, and the ceremony would seem to have been of a semi-magical nature to ensure a successful hunting season. Copal incense was burned, and the feast concluded with the usual ceremonial debauchery.

The following day the fishers held their special feast. It resembled that of the hunters, save that this time the men carried fishing tackle. After the conclusion of the ceremony all repaired to the coast, where they spent the rest of the day fishing and rejoicing. If the feast was half as noisy as a modern Maya festive occasion, one might surmise that the fish would have been frightened away, and the haul consequently small.

Bee-keeping was an important Maya industry, and one is not surprised to find that the bee-keepers, too, had their particular feast. This fell in the month Tzec, the fifth in the year. In this feast, which was dedicated to the Chacs, no blood was drawn from the body and offered. However, the amount of balche wine consumed was particularly large, for one of the chief components of this beverage was honey, and consequently the bee-keepers disposed of large quantities of it.

One of the biggest feasts of the year was held on the day 16 Xul. This was in honor of Kukulcan, the deified Maya and Mexican culture hero. Until the destruction of Mayapan, about eighty years before the arrival of the Spaniards in Yucatan, the ceremony used to be held at this city, which, it was claimed, Kukulcan had founded. After its destruction the feast was transferred to Mani, the new capital of the Xius. This was one of the few Maya ceremonies that can be called national, as most of the others were celebrated by each community independently, although on the same day. However, for the feast of Kukulcan all Yucatan joined together.

Each important city took it in turn to supply four or five magnificent banners of worked feathers. These banners were taken in solemn procession to the temple of Kukulcan, on top of which they were placed. Prior to the feast all the participants had fasted, and they continued to do so till the culmination of the festival, five days later. In the patio in front of the temple each person had his own particular idols placed on special leaves. New fire was next kindled in the manner described for the new year ceremony. Offerings of maize, beans, and calabash seeds, all of which were prepared without salt or chili, were made, and the inevitable copal incense burned. The congregation remained at the feast the whole five days without returning home, spending the time in prayer, and in special religious dances. In the meantime parties of troubadors went from house to house, acting religious plays and collecting money for the feast. The ceremony concluded on the day 1 Yaxkin, five days from the beginning of the feast, when Kukulcan was supposed to descend from the sky and receive the offerings.

In the following month, Mol, there was held a great feast in honor of all the gods. Everything from the temple utensils down to the humble house broom was anointed with the sacred blue. The children, too, were given nine blows on the hands, and were painted blue so that they might grow up to be hard-working useful members of the community.

At this time the new idols of wood were made. This was an arduous and difficult business, owing to the difficulty in shaping the hard wood, as they were made of cedar. The wood was specially brought from the forest, and the work of fashioning it carried on in certain small huts purposely erected. While the work proceeded the artists made continual offerings of copal, and of their own blood, which they drew from their ears and other parts of their bodies. While the work proceeded they were kept shut up in these small huts, and no one was allowed to visit them. They also painted their faces with black paint, this being, as explained above, a sign of fasting and abstinence.

If the idols were being made for private account, the owner rewarded the workers with presents of birds and other foods, and cacao beans, which formed the currency in Yucatan. The new idols were removed to the patio of the hut, where they were blessed by the priest, and after being wrapped up in a cloth were handed over to the owner. The priest then preached a short sermon on the high honor involved in making new idols, and the danger that threatened if the workers did not fast and refrain from sexual intercourse. The ceremony concluded with a big feast and drunken carousal.

Numerous ceremonies were held in honor of the Chacs, the earth gods, who protected the milpas. Of these the most interesting were those held in the month Mac. This feast was made by the older people to ensure good rains and consequently a good harvest. In the middle of the patio of the temple was placed a great bundle of dry sticks. After burning incense, the bundle was set alight, and as soon as it was well alight the people began to throw into the flames the hearts of all the animals and birds they were wont to breed or hunt. If they had no hearts of certain animals, for instance jaguars or large lizards, they used to make imitation hearts fashioned from copal. When all the hearts were burned the four men called Chacs put out the fire with vases of water. This again is an example of sympathetic magic, for thereby it was believed rain would be caused.

The owners of cacoa plantations had their own feast in the month of Muan. The cacao plants were under the special protection of Ek Chuah. The participants proceeded to the plantation of one of the owners, where they sacrificed a dog with markings of the color of cacao beans. In addition they sacrificed blue iguanas and the feathers of a special bird, probably the macaw. This feast was marked by the small quantity of balche wine consumed. The reason for this is probably to be found in the fact that balche drinking was opposed to the consumption of cocoa.

The warriors had their feast in the month Pax. The ceremony was preceded by a five-day vigil in the patio of the temple, as related in the account of the great feast of Kukulcan, save that this feast was in honor of Cit Chac Coh, the red mountain lion, who appears to have been a god of war. The great military leader, the Nacon, was carried to the temple with elaborate pomp, and after being seated was offered gifts and copal incense as though he were divine. For five days this ceremony lasted, while the warriors feasted at the temple and danced war dances. At the end of the five days the

By permission of the Carnegie Institution.

Chichen-Itza. A temple of the pre-Mexican period with masks of the rain
god at the corners.

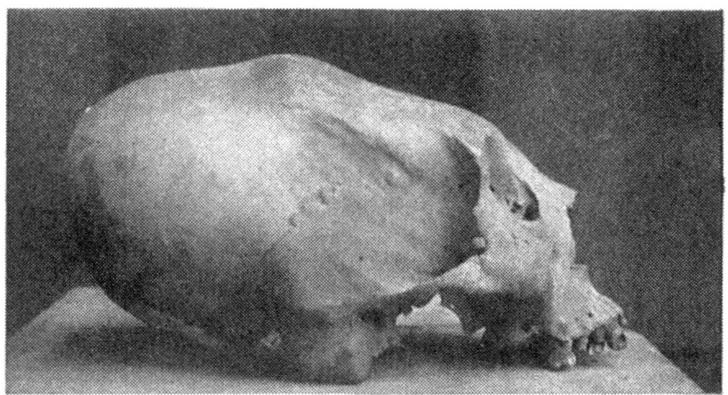

Remarkably deformed Maya skull.

PLATE XV

same ceremony of throwing hearts into the fire as described in the Chac rites was observed, and a dog was sacrificed, his heart being torn out and offered to the gods between two dishes. After that the Chacs broke certain large earthen jars filled with balche wine. The ceremony concluded with the usual feast and drunken debauchery, and the Nacon was carried back to his house, although he had not taken part in the feast, for during his three years of office he was prohibited from indulging the flesh, in order that victory might be attained through his piety.

During the remainder of the year there were a series of fiestas given by different leaders of the community in turn, and the time passed in a long round of ceremonial debaucheries, to such an extent that Bishop Landa writes that it was terrible to see the people going round with their eyes reddened from so much drinking, and with the visible results of their drunken brawls on their persons.

Myths and legends that shed a light on the religious ideas of the Mayas of Yucatan are, unfortunately, almost non-existent. Nevertheless, for the Maya tribes that dwelt in the highlands of Guatemala, there is a mass of legendary tradition and mythology that gives us a considerable insight into the religious outlook of these tribes in particular, and the Maya race in general.

A lucky chance has conserved for posterity the *Popol Vuh*, a mythology and history of the Quichés.

The Quichés are, as explained in Chapter III, a

Maya tribe inhabiting the highlands of Guatemala in the country to the north and west of Lake Atitlan. Shortly after the conquest of the Quichès by Alvarado the cruel, in 1524, the old traditions and history of this people, which had been handed down orally from generation to generation, were put into writing by a native, who had learned from the Spanish priests how to write his own language with European characters. Some fifty years later Francisco Jimenez, a Spanish priest, who spoke fluent Quichè, found this book in use in a Quichè town, where it was being used to instruct the Indian children in their past. Luckily Jimenez was of a more broad-minded nature than most of his contemporaries. He preserved the manuscript, and made a Spanish translation.

In recent years the *Popol Vuh*, as this book was called, has been again translated into Spanish by two distinguished Guatemalan archæologists, Don Antonio Villacorta C. and Don Flavio Rodas V. The short synopsis that follows is based on their translation.

The simplicity and poetry of "The book of our people," as the title means, is well shown in the quoted passages.

The story opens with an account of the first creation. The creator gods, the Mams, are assembled. The world existed, but there was no light, or animal life, as the surface of the world was still below the primeval waters. The creator gods deliberate. "Earth" they say, and the earth is formed. Out of the waters it raised itself up. The creators form the mountains and the valleys, the plants, and the animals and birds. Each is given its allotted place in the world.

The creator gods are vexed as the birds and animals were unable to praise them in intelligible language. They decide to create man. They make men of mud, but the mud is too watery, and will not keep its shape. The first men are a failure. They have no heads, and although they can speak they are unintelligible. Again the creator gods confer, and as a result of their deliberations a fresh race of men is created of wood. They, too, are a failure, and the gods send a flood to drown them. Their domestic animals and utensils, too, attack them.

"On your account our faces are worn away," say the grinding stones: "day after day, at nightfall and dawn, you were always doing to us Holi, holi, huhi, huki (onomatopœic word describing the noise made in grinding corn). That was our task, but now we will try our strength against you."

The dogs in their turn address the wooden men: "How many times through your fault have we not eaten? Only from a distance we dared watch you with fear, we stood before you when you ate, and you threw us out, beating us with your sticks. Thus we were treated without being able to speak to you. Why should we not kill you now?" Thus spoke the dogs.

The wooden men, attacked by their animals and utensils, flee to the house tops, and climb the trees. In vain. The flood sweeps up, and they are drowned. A few survive, and their descendants are the monkeys that one sees in the forest. Thus were the wooden men ended.

After this incident there is an interlude where the adventures of two divine brothers, Hunapu and Xbalanque, are related. Their youth is described, and how they used to wander over the face of the earth with their blowguns, shooting birds for their food. How they destroy three earthquake gods by their superior magic is narrated.

At this time the world was afflicted by three evil giants, who were earthquake gods. These the two brothers decide to kill. The eldest, whose name is Vukub Cakix, is the owner of a nance tree, which he was accustomed to climb to obtain the delicious fruit. One day the brothers espy the god in the top of the tree, busily engaged in plucking the fruit. Hunahpu takes aim at him with his blowgun, hitting him in the mouth. Vukub Cakix, falling out of the tree, rushes to attack his assailants, and in the ensuing struggle, wrenches off one of Hunahpu's arms. With this in his possession he returns home and proceeds to consolidate his victory by magical incantations over the captured arm. In this way he hoped to cause Hunahpu to die.

Realizing the danger he was in, Hunahpu plans to recover his lost arm. Accompanied by two sorcerers, the brothers go disguised to Vukup Cakix, and offer to cure him of his damaged mouth. The giant willingly submits himself to their care, even when they tell him it will be necessary to remove his teeth of precious jewels and substitute grains of maize. Once they have him tied down for the operation, they remove his eyes also, and the giant dies. Hunahpu, recovering his arm, fixes it in position once again, and flushed with success, he and Xbalanque determine to destroy the second giant, Zipacna, Vukup Cakix's son.

The divine brothers start to build a house with the aid of 400 young men. Actually this number should not be translated literally, for 400 is used by the Indians of Central America and Mexico to express innumerable. They are engaged in dragging along a very heavy tree trunk for a corner post, when they meet Zipacna, who offers to help them place it in position. The youths persuade him to get down into the post hole, and then throw logs down on him. The giant is not dead, but to make the brothers think he is, he gives some of his hair and nail parings to ants to take to the surface. The youths, seeing these, believe he is dead and prepare a great feast. In the middle of their rejoicings, Zipacna shakes himself, causing an earthquake, that hurls the 400 youths into the sky, where they become the Pleiades. Hunahpu and Xbalanque escape unharmed.

Zipacna is extremely fond of crabs, and the brothers take advantage of this to destroy him. They make an enormous clay crab, and place it in a large cave under a mountain. Finding Zipacna, they tell him of the enormous crab they have seen, and from the side of the valley they show it to him. Zipacna, not suspecting a trap, enters the cave to get the crab, whereupon the twins destroy him by throwing a mountain on top of him and turning him to stone.

There remains only the third giant, Zipacna's brother, Cabrakan. They shoot a bird with their blow-guns and bake it in poisoned mud. Cabrakan passes by, and smells the sweet smell of the baked fowl, and readily accepts an invitation to partake of it. He is taken very ill and, with the jeers of the brothers in his ears at his lack of strength, expires.

The story then harks back to the adventures of Hunhunahpu and Vukub Hunahpu, who are also two brothers, the father and uncle of Hunahpu and Xbalanque. Hunhunahpu and Vukub Hunahpu are very fond of the ball game described in Chapter VII. The rulers of Xibalba, the underground abode of the dead, invite them to play a match. However, they are first made to pass through a series of ordeals and tests, which appear to have been a form of initiation. In these they fail.

Entering the gloomy house of the rulers of the underworld, they catch sight of two seated figures, which they address. These figures, however, are not human, but wooden statues, and consequently they fail in the first test.

The rulers of Xibalba appear, and bid them be seated, pointing to low benches. The brothers sit down, only to find that the seats are red-hot stones. They have failed in test number two. They pass into the house of gloom, where they are killed and buried. Hunhunahpu's head was hung on a calabash tree, so that in the gloom it looked like a gourd. One day a daughter of one of the rulers of Xibalba chanced to pass close to the tree. Hunhunahpu's head, which still hung on the tree, promptly spits in the girl's outstretched hand, with the result that she becomes pregnant. Escaping to the land of the living, she makes her way to the home of Hunhunahpu's mother, where she gives birth to Hunahpu and Xbalanque.

The story continues with the youth of the two twins, Hunahpu and Xbalanque. Among other things they turn their half brothers into monkeys. One day they learn about the ball game, and that their father's and uncle's equipment is hidden in the house. In order to examine it, they punch a hole in the water jar, so that when their grandmother goes to fetch water, she takes a very long time, as the water pours out of the jar as quickly as it is filled.

They start off for Xibalba to challenge the rulers to a game. On her return their grandmother learns where they have gone, and sends a message to them, warning them of the different ordeals they must undergo. When they get to the hall of reception, they send forward a small ant with a hair from Hunahpu's leg. The ant passes from one figure to another, stinging each seated figure. Those that are human cry out from the pain, and in this way the twins learn which are alive and which of wood. Furthermore, they learn the names of the rulers of Xibalba, and this is a great advantage, for with the knowledge of an opponent's name it is possible to do him harm with black magic. They are also able to avoid the red-hot seats. They are ordered to gather certain flowers, which are well-protected. This they accomplish by sending leaf-cutting ants, which cut the flowers and bring them to the twins. Subsequently they are given cigars, and told they must pass the night smoking them, and still have them alight in the morning. They solve this problem, by catching fireflies, and placing them at the end of their cigars. The rulers of Xibalba, seeing the glow of the fireflies, believe the cigars are still alight, and the twins emerge triumphant. In the last ordeal before the game, misfortune overtakes them. They are required to pass the night in the "House of the Bats."

The "House of the Bats" was, as its name implies, occupied by bats, who would destroy any person who entered. The twins climb into the tubes of their blowguns, and in that way are safe from attack. Just before dawn Hunahpu raises his head to see if the dawn is coming and a bat immediately sweeps down on him and with one lash of his sharp teeth tears off his head.

The twins will not own defeat, for Xbalanque sews a tortoise shell on his brother's shoulders, and then alone goes out to play the rulers of Xibalba. Previously he arranges with a rabbit to help him. The rabbit hides in a hole in the top of the ball-court, and when Xbalanque hits the ball in that direction, the rabbit scuttles out of his hole and down the court. The Xibalbans believe the rabbit to be the ball, run after it, giving Xbalanque time to recover his brother's head and replace it on his shoulders.

Eventually they kill the rulers of Xibalba by trickery. Disguised as wandering entertainers, they kill and then revive themselves several times, in front of the rulers of Xibalba. The rulers of Xibalba are interested, and allow themselves to be killed and brought back to life, but the twins, after killing them, refuse to revive them. The Xibalbans are vanquished and the twins are reunited with their father and uncle. Afterward they ascend to the sky and become the sun and moon.

The story then reverts to the creation. The gods, dissatisfied with their previous attempts, decide to create man afresh.

"Immediately they began to think how they would make and form our first fathers, our first mothers. They made their flesh of the produce of the yellow and white cobs of corn, and their arms and legs they made of the cobs themselves. These were our forefathers. Four in number were the men whom they created from maize."

These new men are intelligent, they speak and act with reason and praise the gods, but they are too intelligent and know as much as their creators. The gods decide to remedy this.

"Then they covered their eyes with a cloth by order of the Heart of Heaven, covering them like the breath covers the surface of a mirror. Thus their eyes became clouded and they could only see what was near."

Afterward four women were created for the first men, and from them are descended all the Indians. Then, at last, the sun rose, for previously the world had been in darkness.

Legends, very similar to the *Popol Vuh*, are still current among the Kekchis of the Alta Vera Paz region of Central Guatemala, and the Mopan Indians to the north of them. The whole cycle of legends deals with these two mythical heroes of the Mayas, who became, afterward, the sun and the morning star, or, if one is to accept the *Popal Vuh* on this point, the sun and the moon. In turn they link up with a series of legends of the two brothers current all over the new world from the United States to the Argentine. In fact the *Popol Vuh* has its origins in the dawn of new world history, long before the Maya civilization had developed.

CHAPTER VII

DAILY LIFE, WARFARE, FOOD, AND
CLOTHING
(J. E. T.)

Casting the horoscope at birth. Skull deformation in the infant very prevalent amongst the Maya. Artificial production of squint in children. Depilation. Ceremonies in which boys and girls took part to insure their growing up hard workers. Education of children of the lower classes and of the nobility. Marriage ceremonies. The husband had to serve his father-in-law for several years after marriage. Widows had only to get a widower to eat in their house in order to forge the bond of matrimony. Monogamy. Punishment of adultery. Mourning the dead. Burial customs amongst the nobles and the poorer classes. Laws of inheritance. Method of choosing chiefs. The game of Tlaxtli and the method of playing it. Other games. The Maya were great gamblers. The rise of the Maya against the Spaniards in 1847. Weapons used by the Maya were bows and arrows, spears, slings, and swords. Defensive armor and shields. Method of making war. Officers of the army, and its constitution. Dances. Music. Ceremonial feasts. Foodstuffs. Fermented drinks. Clothes and ornaments worn by the nobles, priests, and common people. Tattooing and skin painting and stamping. Tooth filing and inlaying. Hairdressing. Houses and furniture of the nobles and the lower classes. Sweat houses. The great ruined cities were really religious centres. Maya calendar more accurate than the Julian calendar. Mistakes occurring on the monuments, Their possible reason. Maya monuments erected purely for scientific purposes.

THE whole life of the Maya from childhood to death centred round two things, which in turn were closely allied—religion and agriculture. The day on which a child was born was carefully noted, and later the priest of the community cast the child's horoscope according to the position of that day in the sacred calendar of 260 days. In fact his future life was to a large extent governed by this accident of birth. Persons born on one day had to avoid certain things all through their lives, or they would be unlucky or lucky according to the day on which they were born. In fact, in many cases the children were named after the day on which they were born.

Four or five days after birth the child was placed mouth downward on a small cradle constructed of wooden boards. A board was then tied to the back of the head, and another to the forehead, and these two boards were tightly lashed together. The object of this practice was to cause the child's head to take a sugar-loaf shape, as the only direction in which the head could grow was upwards. The Mayas considered this shape of head a mark of beauty. Numerous examples of this type of what might be termed Maya classical beauty are to be seen on the sculptured lintels and stelæ of the Old Empire, that clearly show the receding foreheads forming an almost straight line with the noses.

Squinting, too, was considered a mark of beauty, and was deliberately caused by the mothers, who suspended some small object from the child's hair, so that it dangled down between the eyebrows, and caused the squint to form. Beards were not esteemed as a mark of beauty, and again the mothers interfered with the course of nature, scalding the faces of the boys with

Courtesy of the Field Museum

A magnificent stela at Copan. Note the dress with diamond pattern

Chichen-Itza. Back view of a temple of the pre-Mexican period; showing the flying façade from behind

PLATE XVI

hot cloths to prevent the growth of hair. However, the American Indians are by nature a hairless race, and their lack of beards probably had little to do with this maternal treatment.

When a boy reached the age of four months, he underwent a ceremonial introduction to the cares and worries of life. He was led to a small tree, and an axe was placed in his hand. An adult then guided his hand so that he went through the motions of cutting down the tree. Afterward he was made to go through the actions of an ordinary adult man engaged in his daily work. This was to ensure that he grew up to be a hard worker, and in particular a good agriculturist. The ceremony was held at the end of four uinals (months) because four was the sacred number associated with the milpa, four being the number of the chief earth gods, who protected the crops. Only after this ceremony could the boy be carried by his mother astraddle her hip. A similar ceremony was undergone by the girls. In their case they were made to go through the actions of grinding corn, of weaving, etc. However, this ceremony took place when they were three months old, because three is woman's sacred number, as their work is associated with the fire and cooking, and the hearth stones are three in number.

Children were not weaned until they were about three years old. In early life they went about naked. However, when they reached the age of four or five the boys were given a small loin cloth, and the girls wore a shell. At the age of about twelve or so they underwent the ceremonial reception into the adult community described in Chapter VI. After this the boys went to live in a large house, which all the young unmarried men frequented for sports, and as sleeping quarters. The girls were then free to marry. However, until after marriage the young people continued to help their parents in their work, the boys going to work with their fathers in the milpas, the girls remaining at home to aid in the housework. Sons of the nobility were given a more thorough education, being assembled in special houses, where they received instruction in the religious ceremonies, astrology, history, and the calendar, from special priests. Similarly daughters of the nobility were received into special communities where they were placed under the guidance of the Maya equivalent of the mother superior of a convent. Among the duties that devolved upon them while members of these convents were the sweeping and cleaning of the temples and the care of the sacred fire. Any lapse of chastity during this period was punished by death, but the girls were free to leave the convents and marry whenever their parents might decide; in fact, this was the common rule.

Maya parents had one peculiar method of punishing refractory children. They would rub chili pepper onto the child's bare skin. This causes an intense sensation of burning.

Young men usually married when about twenty years

old, the girls being as a rule a few years younger. Marriages were not the outcome of a romantic wooing, but were arranged by the parents with the aid of professional matchmakers. The parents of a young man usually sought an eligible bride in their own community; however, marriage between persons of the same name was forbidden, although cousins, if not of the same name, could marry. When the match had been arranged the father of the young man made a present to the girl's parents, and the mother, in addition, made clothes for her son and future daughter-in-law. The young man, too, had to supply his bride-to-be with food from the time the couple were betrothed.

The wedding ceremony itself was a simple affair. It was held in the house of the bride's parents, the priest of the community officiating. After first assuring himself that all parties were agreeable to the match, he gave the girl to the young man, and the ceremony concluded with a big feast. The young couple took up residence with the wife's parents, the husband paying for his wife by working for her father for the next five or six years. After that period he was free to set up house on his own account. A widow could get herself a new husband, if she could persuade a widower to come to her house and eat there, that being all the ceremony required of those that had previously married.

Polygamy was not practised by the Mayas; nevertheless, they were very prone to desert their wives, and go to live with some other woman. When a couple thus separated, the children, if they were small, remained with their mother, but if they were of some age, the sons went to live with their father, while the daughters remained with their mother.

Despite this looseness of the marriage bond, adultery was a very serious offence. In Mayapan a man found guilty of adultery was tied to a post and then turned over to the woman's husband to do as he liked with. He could either forgive the adulterer, or he could kill him by dropping a heavy stone on his head. The woman was not punished so harshly, but was considered to suffer sufficiently from the loss of the respect of the community. The women were, and are to this day, in a very inferior position in the community as compared with the men. They were not admitted to the big feasts in the temples, and they ate apart from men, even their own husbands. Laughing at a man was considered a sign of looseness, and if a woman met a man coming along a path, she would get off the path, and turn her back on him until he had passed. Nevertheless women, like their husbands, frequently got drunk, although only at their own feasts to which women only were admitted. They were extremely jealous, and thought nothing of fighting another woman whom they considered to be stealing their husband's affection.

The death of a person was mourned by all the deceased's relatives. By day the mourners wept in silence, but at night they indulged in loud and long lamentations. All mourners fasted for some period after the

death, and covered themselves with a black sooty substance, with which they always painted themselves when
fasting. In the mouth of the deceased were placed
grains of maize and, in the case of the wealthier people,
a piece of jade. The dead man's dog was killed and
buried with him, as the dog guided him on his journey
to the next world. In addition to this the man's possessions were buried with him, his spear, bowls of food,
clothing, jewellery, etc., so that he might continue to
live in the next world as he had lived in this. In the
same way with a sorcerer were buried his medical implements, with a high priest his books, and with a woman
her household possessions, such as her corn grinder and
weaving utensils.

Persons of rank were often buried in or at the foot of
pyramids, but the ordinary rank and file found their
last resting place behind or under the floor of the hut
they had occupied during life. After such a burial the
hut was usually abandoned from fear of the spirit of
the deceased, but if there were a number of occupants
they would sometimes find courage in their numbers to
remain.

In some parts of the Maya area the nobles were
cremated, and a temple built over the urn in which the
ashes were placed. Another interesting method of dis-
posing of the dead was in vogue among some of the
nobility. Part of the body was burned, and the ashes
were placed in hollow wooden statuettes, which had an
opening at the back of the neck. The aperture was sub-

sequently sealed by the corresponding piece of skin removed from the dead man's body. The rest of the body was interred, but the statuette was kept in the hut in a place of honor.

The Cocoms, one of the ruling families of Yucatan, cut off the head of any member of their family who died. The head was boiled and all the flesh thus removed. The skull was then sawn from top to bottom, and the front half covered with wax, which was modelled to the dead man's features. Subsequently the head was placed in the family temple, and offerings were made to it on the occasion of important feasts.

In British Honduras secondary burial was frequently practised, the bodies being first exposed, possibly in a tree, and then buried several in one grave, or in large urns. Burials are found of almost every conceivable type with the bodies lying face downward, or upward, on the side, or squatting with the knees drawn up to the chin. In some parts elaborate vaulted chambers, often with stairs leading down into them, served as the last resting places of leaders of the community.

On the death of a man, his property was divided up equally among the sons, unless one of them had been more instrumental than the others in helping his father to amass the property, in which case that son received a larger share than the others. Daughters were not entitled to any inheritance, but in actual fact they were often given a share. If the sons were too young to inherit, guardians were appointed till they came of age.

Courtesy of the Field Museum

PLATE XVII. POTTERY FIGURINE WHISTLE FROM THE
USUMACINTLA VALLEY

The woman is carrying a fire fan. There is a two-hole whistle at the back.
Note the ear-plugs

In the event of there being no sons, but only daughters, the deceased's brother inherited the property. A chief was usually succeeded by his eldest son, but if a younger son appeared to have more ability, he might be elected chief.

Most Maya families of position possessed slaves, theft being punished by slavery. In time of famine it is said that there was a great increase in the number of slaves, a large number of free men being caught stealing food to live, and suffering the punishment of slavery. Slaves were also recruited from prisoners of war, although these latter, if young and of rank, were usually sacrificed.

The most important game played by both the Mayas and the Mexicans was the Tlaxtli, as it was called by the Mexicans. This was played in a long court, which varied in size, but might be as much as 190 yards long and forty yards wide. The court was enclosed by high walls, and the ground plan was in the form of two T's placed base to base. Teams stood at each end, playing with a hard rubber ball, the object of the game being to drive the ball through two rings set high up, one in the middle of each of the side walls. This was considered very difficult, and in Mexico, at least, any player who succeeded in accomplishing it was allowed to take the clothes of any of the onlookers, who watched from the flat tops of the walls. The ball was either hit with the hand or, when particularly skillful players were engaged, with the hips, which were protected by a pad, hands not being allowed. The game was intimately bound up with religion, and often a special temple was built adjoining the court, where the players sacrificed before and after playing. The game was said to have been introduced by the gods and around it centred a regular cult. The largest and best preserved ball-court is that at Chichen. There are temples at both ends and a third and very elaborately decorated temple is perched on top of one of the walls. The players were probably confined to those of noble rank.

A number of other games were popular among the rank and file, and gambling was very rife. The favorite gambling game was played with grains of maize, which were painted with black marks and thrown into the air. The scoring depended on the way they fell. Equally popular among the Mexicans, and presumably among the Mayas too, was a game not unlike our children's game of ludo. This was played with beans on a board marked like a Saint Andrew's cross. The Mayas were, and are to this day, inveterate gamblers, and it was by no means uncommon for a Maya to gamble away all his possessions, and eventually lose his liberty in a vain effort to recoup his losses.

The Mayas appear to have been on the whole a fairly peaceful people, not much addicted to warfare, but once roused a cruel and ruthless foe. The history of Yucatan in the middle of the nineteenth century bears out this estimate. In 1847 the Mayas, after three centuries of heartless persecution and enslavement, rose in rebellion against the whites and half-castes under the leadership of two natural leaders, Jacinto Pat and Cecilio Chi. At first the Maya forces comported themselves according to all the rules of civilized warfare, but the white troops, who claimed to be protecting civilization against the hordes of barbarism, started shooting down peaceful Mayas, raping young girls, and burning whole Maya villages and towns. The Mayas took a fearful vengeance for these atrocities and for the three centuries of cruel oppression they had endured, and for eighteen months Yucatan suffered a series of appalling atrocities and excesses committed by both sides. Victory was within the grasp of the Mayas, when the time for preparing the milpas arrived. The Mayas, unable to resist the eternal call of the soil, deserted the army, when the whole of Yucatan had been conquered and only the capital Merida remained unsubdued. The army melted away like that of the Assyrians, and the Maya cause was lost.

There is no information as to whether the Mayas of the Old Empire fought among themselves, except that on many of the stone monuments are to be seen captives with arms bound behind their backs, ready for the sacrificial block. The presumption is that these were captives taken in warfare, for such was the custom in later times, as explained below.

In the century that preceded the arrival of the Spaniards in their territory, the Mayas were engaged in a series of internecine wars, that rent the country and did much to facilitate the Spanish Conquest. Central rule disappeared under the centrifugal urge, that exists all through Central America, and Yucatan was partitioned off into a large number of small states continually at war with one another.

The principal weapon of the Mayas was the bow and arrow, but this appears to have been a fairly recent innovation among them, having been introduced probably from Mexico. Each bowman went into battle with two quivers of arrows apiece. In addition to bows and arrows the Mayas used spears, which were propelled by means of spearthrowers. The spearthrower, which enables greater distance and force to be attained, was introduced into Yucatan from Mexico, although it would appear to have been known in the Old Empire. Slings were also employed to hurl stones at the enemy, as well as a weapon, resembling a top, which was hurled by means of a string wound round it. There is also certain evidence, which would point to the Mayas having been acquainted with the returning boomerang. For close fighting the Mayas possessed long swords, which were grasped with both hands. They were made of hard wood, and into the sides were set at intervals blades of obsidian. They were about three and a half feet long.

For defence the Mayas used shields made of sticks over which were placed tiger or deer skins. These shields were either square or round, and in addition long flexible shields, possibly made of thickly plaited rush, were sometimes used. However, the chief protection was afforded by a kind of cotton quilt, which was worn like armor, and covered the whole body from the neck to below the knees. These quilts were nearly three inches thick, and seem to have served their purpose very well until the introduction by the Spaniards of steel weapons.

The Mayas also made use of all possible psychological aids to victory. Warriors painted their faces black, white and red, and in addition endeavored to frighten their enemies by means of shouts, hisses, the beating of drums, and the blowing of conch shells. However, there was a great deal of ceremony attached to warfare. No fight was supposed to commence until compliments had been exchanged between the opposing forces. Aychuykak, the god of war, was carried into battle by four captains on a special litter.

Warriors went into battle decked in their finest feather headdresses. In addition they carried banners made of feather mosaics. Ambuscades were a common feature of warfare, the soldiers lying in wait at the side of a road through the forest and then, to the accompaniment of yells, hurling themselves on the enemy. Presumably war was declared and the first battle fought with full ceremony, but afterward for the rest of the campaign, surprise was permitted. However, night warfare was unknown to the Mayas, as well as to most of the Mexican peoples.

A special effort was made to capture as many of the enemy as possible, as captives of rank were destined for human sacrifice, while the rest were enslaved. A warrior who killed an opponent took the dead man's jaw-bone, and removing the flesh, wore it as a trophy on his arm.

The army was led by two generals, one of whom held a permanent position, while the other was elected to his post for a period of three years. He was known as Nacon, and was held in special honor and esteem. On him fell the duty of arranging the special warriors' feast held in the month Pax. During the whole three years he had to fast, and live apart from women. During this period, he was not allowed to get drunk, nor eat meat, but he was allowed to eat fish and iguana meat.

The army was composed of a kind of permanent militia. During peace time the soldiers carried on with their ordinary civilian occupations, living at home just like any other member of the community, and receiving no pay. However, in time of war they were summoned to fight, and during their time with the army they were paid a small salary, which came either from the personal funds of the captain, or from the villages in which they lived. The women, too, were pressed into service to prepare the food. After the close of hostilities they were demobilized, returning to their villages, where they were fêted if they had distinguished themselves in the war, and in particular if they had killed or captured an enemy of rank. Nevertheless they, like all soldiers through the ages, were inclined to be arrogant, and unruly after demobilization.

The Mayas were very much addicted to dancing, but dances in which both sexes took part were extremely rare. Probably the most interesting of the men's dances was that associated with the extinguishing of the burner, a religious ceremony that occurred every fifty-two days. A large fire was made, and as soon as it began to die down the hot embers were smoothed off so as to cover a large space. The high priest then walked over the burning embers barefoot and dressed in a long white dress made of the bark of a tree. As he went he scattered on the flames the intoxicant known as balche. As soon as the priest had crossed, all the men began to run and dance across the embers. Apparently the men did not suffer any burns on their feet, but the performance was not a hoax as is shown by the statement of an observer that sometimes a drunken Indian would lose his balance, and falling down, lie in a drunken stupor, until he burned to death. A similar dance is performed in many parts of Oceania.

Another interesting dance resembled the folk-dances of the Russians. The dancers formed a circle, and two of their number danced in the centre. One of them was armed with a number of reed lances which he hurled with all his might at his partner, who, dancing as he squatted, parried them one by one with a small shield no wider than a pole. Many of the dances were magical in origin, and had as their object the cajoling of the powers of nature. To such a class belong hunting and agricultural dances to ensure plenty of game or good harvests.

For music the Mayas possessed a number of different instruments, most of which were not, however, very effective. There were three different types of drums made of hollowed wood, and these were beaten with rubber-tipped drum sticks. The largest type, which was horizontal with a slit in the wood along the top, was said to have been audible at a distance of six miles. Turtle carapaces were beaten with deer antlers, and large conch shells were used as trumpets, the top being sawed off. Four-holed flutes of wood, reed, bone, or pottery were also used, as also whistles, the fronts of which were often carved or moulded in the form of gods, warriors, or animals. Simple wooden trumpets with mouthpieces made of calabash, and rattles helped to swell the orchestra, and in addition the musical bow with its string made of henequen cord was employed. However, on the whole not much real music was achieved, the result being for the most part rhythm plus much noise. There appears to have been a kind of tribal copyright in songs, for we are told that in Guatemala songs formed part of the tribute paid.

The Maya nobles entertained themselves and each other with frequent banquets, which were the occasion for much rivalry in ostentation and hospitality. These banquets were confined to men, although women, too, had their own feasts to which only their sex was admitted. The guests to a banquet had at some future date to return the hospitality, unless they were of the same family, and should a guest die before he had had an opportunity of returning the entertainment he had received, his heirs were responsible for the payment of the debt of hospitality.

The banquets were frequently very costly affairs, the host spending in the entertainment of his guests a small fortune. The guests sat at small low tables for two or four persons. After the conclusion of the meal, the guests were served cups of honey wine until they were intoxicated. The wives of the guests waited outside to conduct their drunken husbands home. The Mayas, nevertheless, when drunk, are an extremely quarrelsome race, and then, as now, numerous fights and brawls occurred, the men sometimes even burning down their own houses in their drunken frenzy.

Each guest to a banquet was presented by his host with a cloak of cotton or feather mosaic work, in addition to a small wooden stool and a painted pottery vase.

Although the Mayas lacked many of the common foods to which we are accustomed, wheat, rice, potatoes, bananas, oats, etc., nevertheless they possessed a large number of fruits, meats and vegetables from which to choose. The Maya staff of life was maize, and no meal was complete without it served in some form or other. Maize was usually eaten in the form of griddle cakes, known to-day under the Spanish name "tortillas." The maize, after being shelled, was left to soak over-night in a solution of lime and water. In the morning it was rinsed in clean water and then ground on a rubbing stone. These rubbing stones were oblong in shape and had a concave surface. The grains were ground on this concave surface with the "hand," a stone roller, which tended to be oval in cross-section. As soon as the maize was ground to a fine paste the woman, for all cooking was woman's work, took some of the dough and with her fingers kneaded it until a thin pancake was formed. These cakes were placed on a pottery griddle to bake over a slow-burning fire. The tortillas were eaten much as we eat bread, but often, among the poor people, dipped in chili pepper, they formed the chief article of diet.

Maize was also employed in making tamales of meat, beans, or calabash seeds. These did not differ to any marked extent from those served in many restaurants in this country, except that they contained a much higher percentage of chili pepper. Maize was also the basis for many drinks, serving as a gruel or, fermented, as an intoxicant. For long journeys balls of maize paste were made, which, on being mixed with water, supplied a beverage that both quenched thirst and assuaged hunger.

The list of fruits and vegetables grown by the Mayas is lengthy. The sweet potato, sweet mandioc, tomatoes, and a number of varieties of squashes and beans were cultivated, as well as numerous fruits such as the papaya, the avocado pear, plums, various types of anonas, the fruit of the breadnut tree, and the highly important cacao bean.

Cacao was highly prized by the Mayas, as indeed all

the ancient peoples of Central America. The beans were roasted ground and boiled with ground maize and chili pepper. Before serving the drink was frothed with an elaborately carved wooden swivel stick. The consumption of cacao was so great in Yucatan that large quantities of the bean were imported from Tabasco. The beans served also as money.

The vast majority of the people were agriculturists. According to Bishop Landa, each family was allotted a space of 400 square yards for agricultural purposes. This must surely be a mistake, for it would be impossible to raise sufficient crops on an area of this size in rocky barren Yucatan. Probably Landa meant to say that each family had a plot of land of this size in the vicinity of the town, in which to raise fruit and vegetables, but a larger extension some way away, where maize, beans, and squashes were grown.

Land was laid out with a measure called a "kan" or cord length, which is roughly 400 square yards, and was probably based on twenty paces each way. Throughout Central America agricultural land is still measured by this same cord-length measure. The Mayas still use their term "kan," but the Spanish-speaking population use the corrupted Aztec term "mecate," which has the same meaning and is the same length.

The Mayas had, and in fact still have, the custom of banding together in groups of sixteen or twenty to aid one another in preparing the land and sowing the crops, working in turn on the land of each member of the group. The head of each family chose a section of the forest where he wished to plant his crops. Usually a new piece of ground was chosen each year, as the growth of thorny scrub after clearing made work very difficult on the same piece of land two years in succession. After an interval of six to ten years the land had recovered its fertility, the thorny scrub had been replaced by better growth, and the land was ready for cultivation once more.

The night before work commenced was spent in vigil and feasting, no member of the group being allowed to sleep. Early in the morning the group repaired to the chosen spot. Prayers were said and copal incense offered to the earth gods, and then the work of cutting down the forest commenced. This must have been a laborious business, as the Mayas had no implement better than a stone axe, although these were supplanted to a certain extent by hatchets of soft copper shortly before the arrival of the Spaniards. However, the hard work of chopping down the big trees was, to a certain extent, circumvented by first circling the barks of the trees with fire so that they died.

As soon as the land of one member was cleared the whole group passed on to the land chosen by some other member of the group, continuing in this manner until the land of all the members of the group had been prepared. The trees and scrub, after being cut down, were left to dry under the strong rays of the tropical vernal sun. Early in April the clearing was ready to be burned. This, too, was the occasion of another vigil, and prayers and copal were offered to the wind gods so that they would "play with the flames" and cause the dry brush to burn well.

Just before the first rains were expected the seed was sown. The method employed was simple. The sower walked across the land with a sack of seed and a sharp-pointed stick. Making a hole in the ground, he dropped three or four grains of maize in it, subsequently covering up the hole and heaping a little earth on top with his foot. Both before sowing and while the crop was still new the owner continuously prayed for a good harvest. During this period, too, he abstained from all sexual intercourse.

While the crops were growing and needed little attention the people were probably conscripted for work on the pyramids and temples. In all probability even the women and children took part in this work, carrying rocks and earth with the aid of a head-strap.

Harvest was the occasion of general rejoicing and thanksgiving. The first fruits of the soil were offered to the earth gods. A hole was dug in the ground, which, after being lined with stones, was heated by a fire built inside it. As soon as the stones were well heated the fire was taken out, the new maize put in and the hole covered with earth. In a short while the food was cooked and ready to be offered to the gods, who had given the harvest.

For meat the Mayas were largely dependent on

hunting. Game, such as wild boar, deer, or coati, was obtained either by hunting with bow and arrow with the aid of dogs, or by means of deadfall or noose traps. Blowguns were largely used for shooting birds. These were from six to ten feet long and made of hollowed wood. The poisoned darts associated with the blowgun in South America appear to have been unknown to the Mayas, who in their stead used small clay pellets, into which were occasionally inserted sharpened bone points.

In Yucatan the turkey had been domesticated, as well as other closely allied birds, and in Guatemala the macaw, and probably the quetzal bird as well, were bred for their feathers. There is a certain amount of evidence, too, that herds of deer were kept in captivity, but dogs were certainly raised for eating purposes. The Indians of Central America were very partial to dog, and we read accounts by the early Spaniards of regular herds, which were bred just as we breed cattle, the females being kept for breeding purposes, the males, which were gelded, being fattened up for consumption. There were two breeds of dogs. One breed appears to have been a kind of small greyhound, which were used as watch dogs and for hunting. The dogs that were preferred for eating were a small hairless variety, which were said not to have been able to bark. Dogs, as already noted, were also frequently sacrificed to the gods in various religious ceremonies.

The Mayas, too, had domesticated the stingless bee. The hives consisted of long wooden tubes or hollowed

Maya female costume

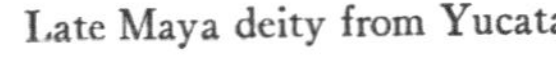

Late Maya deity from Yucatan

Plate XVIII

tree trunks stopped up at each end with mud, and with a small hole in the side for the bees to enter and leave the hive. The bee-keepers had their own patron god, who was invoked on special occasions. The modern bee-keepers of Yucatan still have their special ceremonies for the lord of the bees.

The honey was chiefly employed in the preparation of balche, the ceremonial drink. The honey was mixed with the shavings from the bark of a tree of the genus *lonchocarpus*, which were first bruised. After being left three days the mixture was sufficiently fermented to supply a mild intoxicant, much relished by the Mayas.

In addition to the food-stuffs grown in their milpas, the Mayas raised large quantities of cotton for clothing and for export, when woven, to Tabasco and the coast of Honduras.

The usual clothing worn by the men consisted of a waist girdle, which passed between the legs. The ends, which hung down back and front, were elaborately embroidered with colored thread or feather mosaic work. A kind of mantle, which was square in shape, was draped over the shoulders, and the feet were protected by sandals made of hide. Members of the nobility wore more elaborate clothes of the same shape, but in addition they decked themselves with feather mosaic head-dresses, jade breast ornaments, and belts and sandals studded with jade, or in later times gold. Armlets and leglets were also worn by those of rank. However, the most prized possession of a member of the Maya nobility was his head-dress of quetzal feathers. The quetzal bird is found only in the highlands of Guatemala, and these feathers had to be imported into Yucatan and most of the Old Empire cities, and consequently were extremely precious, in addition to being sacred.

Priests wore long dresses that reached to the ankles, made either of bark cloth or cotton. The bark of certain trees was stripped off and softened by hammering and washing in water until it was sufficiently pliable to be used as clothing. A nineteenth-century English writer described this bark cloth as being soft as wash-leather.

Members of the nobility also wore on special occasions cloaks of feathers. The feathers were sown one by one onto a cloth back, and were arranged according to colors so as to form delicate patterns. The feathers of macaws were so treated, and we are told that the Mayas bred special birds for the sake of their feathers. Nobles, in addition to these special garments, were further differentiated from the rank and file by their use of nose ornaments and lip- and ear-plugs.

Of these forms of decoration ear-plugs were the commonest. At an early age the lobe of the ear was pierced and a small circular jade ornament inserted. This was held in position either by a carved bone skewer or by small transversal sticks in the back of the phlange of the ornament. The orifice made in the ear was gradually enlarged, each time larger ornaments being placed in the lobes of the ears, until jade ear-plugs as much as five to six inches wide were used. Women, too, wore ear-plugs of a similar size to those used by the men. Poorer people, who could not afford or were not permitted jade, had to be content with ear-plugs or even beads of pottery. Nose ornaments of various types were used, the material being jade, amber, and in later times gold.

The Mayas of both sexes were fond of tattooing their faces with elaborate designs, and the women also tattooed their breasts, which in most parts were exposed, as the skirts they wore reached only to the base of their chests. Besides tattooing their bodies, the Mayas used to paint designs on their bodies by means of pottery stamps engraved with special designs, which they applied to their skins after dipping them in vegetable and mineral paints. Finally, in addition to the head deformation and squinting described in a previous chapter, the Mayas beautified themselves by filing or inlaying their front teeth. Teeth were filed in a number of different ways. Sometimes they were filed to a point, while on other occasions all the front teeth were filed down in a straight line about quarter of an inch except the adjacent halves of the two centre teeth, which were left untouched, thereby forming a small square, which jutted out from the line of the filed teeth. The inlays usually consisted of small circular plugs of iron pyrites, obsidian, or occasionally jade, which were let into the centre of the teeth by drilling small circular holes. This was the work of special old women, although both sexes were so decorated.

Warriors had the crowns of their heads burned, but the hair of the back of the head was gathered into a queue, which was wound round the head and the end left hanging down behind. Many of the men wore a kind of fringe in front, which was held upright by a band of cotton or bark cloth. Women wore their hair long, with the same fringe affected by many of the men. They also plaited their hair into two or four plaits. The complete cropping of the hair was considered a degradation, and was reserved as a method of punishing crimes that did not merit death or slavery, as there was no such thing as imprisonment. In the same way a prisoner, who had been accused of a serious crime, and whose guilt, although strongly suspected, could not be proved, suffered the same punishment.

Members of the nobility had their houses in the town, where resided the ruler of the district. At the time that the whole of Yucatan was united under the rulership of Mayapan all the chiefs of the country resided in that city. The houses were not unlike those still in use in Yucatan at the present time. The roofs were made of palm leaf, and the house itself was divided into two principal rooms by a transversal wall. The back room served as the sleeping quarters, and the front room as the living and reception room. The front room, however, was open in front, partaking more of the nature of a verandah. The wall between the two rooms was covered with stucco, on which were painted frescos of a naturalistic or religious nature. There was little fur-

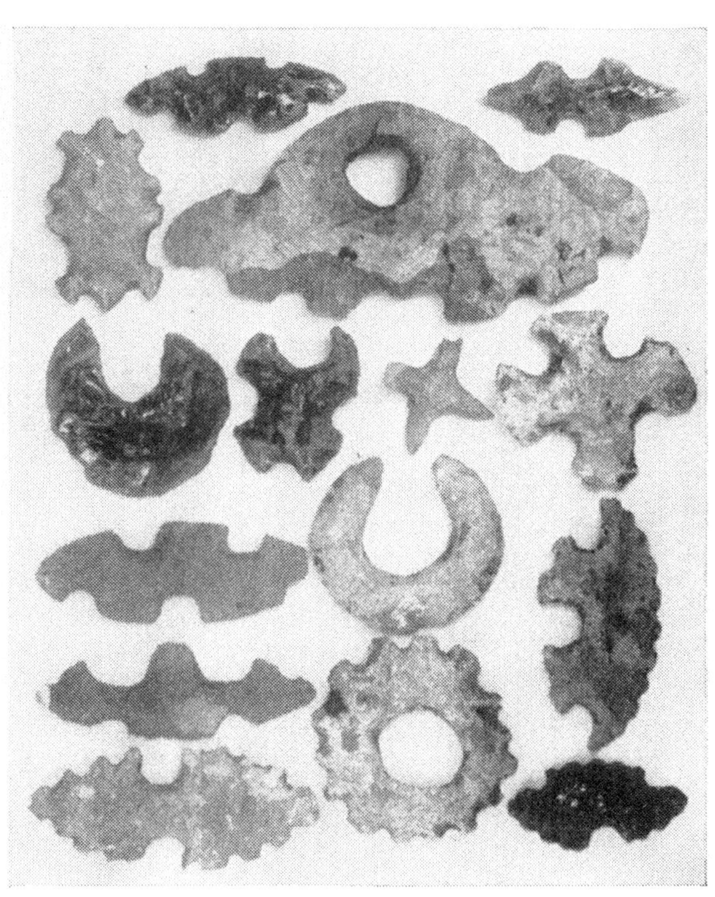

PLATE XIX.   PUSILHA: FLINT AND OBSIDIAN ECCENTRIC
OBJECTS FOUND BESIDE THE BASE OF STELA E

niture. Small stools and, in all probability, hammocks served as seats, and low tables and mats completed the furniture of the front room. The back room contained the beds on which the people slept. They were made of thin pieces of wood, over which were laid rush mats. Cotton blankets were used during the cold season.

The cottages of the common people were of the same general nature as those of the nobles, but more poorly constructed, lacking the stucco on the walls. The houses were usually oblong in shape, with the corners slightly rounded, but circular huts were not entirely unknown. In fact, circular huts are still used by certain Maya peoples in the State of Chiapas. The Mayas of this region and the highlands of Guatemala also made use of sweat houses. These were small oven-shaped constructions daubed with clay or stucco, which were used for both religious and medical purposes. They were heated by hot stones.

The agriculturists lived in small settlements of a few families, scattered through the forest, and fairly close to their plantations. For each area there was a religious centre, to which the people repaired for the different feasts and sacrifices when summoned by their priests. In fact the common people, it may be assumed, never lived in the big so-called ruined cities. These were of an almost purely religious nature, and were inhabited only by the more important priests, and possibly a few of the civil leaders. The villagers had to keep these religious and civil leaders supplied with all the necessities of life, and were also called upon to construct the temples and dwelling houses for them.

The common people probably resorted to the big centres for justice. If the defendant and the petitioner were from different communities, justice was dispensed by the chief of the community to which the defendant belonged. As explained above, imprisonment as a punishment was unknown. Slavery was frequently the punishment meted out for a serious offense, but for petty offenses a fine was usually imposed on the culprit, payable in cotton mantles, cacao seeds, etc. If the defendant was unable to pay, his relations used to club together and pay the fine for him, the matter being looked upon as something in the way of a family debt of honor. Offenses against family morality have already been dealt with in the discussion of marriage; however, unnatural vice was punished by the burning alive of the guilty ones. Homicide, if unintentional, was punished with a fine, and this, too, was the punishment for accidental arson, the fine corresponding to the amount of damage done.

With the population divided into priests, nobles, and warriors on the one side and the common people on the other, there was little room for a middle class. However, if we could apply such a term to the aboriginal civilizations of Central America, we might say that the merchants formed the middle class. Although looked down upon by the warrior class, they possessed certain privileges, and like the merchants of mediæval Europe they were banded in guilds. Merchants were recognized by their badge of office—a fan, a symbol of travel. Their mistreatment by a foreign people was considered a very serious crime, and a pretext for war among the Mexicans, and probably the same applied among the Mayas. Merchants were often absent several months on a business trip, and both before setting forth and while en route they commended themselves to the special protection of the god of cacao. As already explained, the reason for this god being their patron lay in the fact that cacao beans were the universal currency of Central America.

Few of the Maya cities were well located for raw materials. In the limestone area of the Peten and Yucatan no minerals are found, and flint was almost the only stone found in any abundance. Obsidian, which together with flint was universally used for knives, spear points, sword blades, etc., was imported in large quantities from the south, probably from the mines situated close to the modern town of Zacapa in Guatemala. Jade and allied green stones were highly prized by all the Central American peoples. They were imported from southwest Mexico and possibly the adjacent regions of Guatemala. Turquoise, too, was imported, although this was always a great rarity among the Mayas. It is possible that it may have been brought from as far away as the mines of New Mexico. Copper, gold, and silver, though unknown in the Old Empire, were imported into Yucatan during the two or three hundred years that preceded the Spanish Conquest. The gold in most cases appears to have come from the area lying between Costa Rica and Panama. In some cases the objects were imported already worked, in other cases the raw material was obtained and the fashioning done by Maya goldsmiths.

The copper used was probably obtained from the Zapotecs of Oaxaca. In what is to-day the Republic of El Salvador a certain clay, heavily impregnated with lead, was used in making pottery. After firing the vessels assumed a kind of glazed surface, apparently much prized by the different peoples of Central America. These vessels in certain specialized shapes were exported far and wide. They have been found at Chichen-Itza and other cities of Yucatan, at Copan, and all over the highlands of Guatemala, in Vera Cruz, the Valley of Mexico, and as far away as Jalisco on the west coast of Mexico.

In return the Mayas of Yucatan exported large quantities of embroidered cotton mantles, for which Yucatan was famous. Exquisitely carved jade and mother-of-pearl shell were exported from the cities of the Old Empire, and have been found in cities as far distant as Tula and Teotihuacan in central Mexico. The jade in these cases was imported unworked and then re-exported in a finished condition. The Mayas of Yucatan also, apparently, paid for their imports with slaves, and possibly honey as well.

In addition to this trade, which might be denominated international, there was a considerable amount of internal trade. Salt was an important commodity, and from the workings near Silan on the north coast of Yucatan salt was sent over a large area. Sea shells, too, are commonly found in inland cities, and must have been traded. Economic warfare was not unknown, for we are told that the Cocoms, who controlled the area around Silan, refused to let their enemies the Chels have any supplies of salt. The Chels, as noted in the chapter dealing with the history of Yucatan, replied by forbidding the export of cacao beans from their territory to that of the Cocoms.

Trading was carried on both by land and by sea, and it is not without the bounds of possibility that the Mayas of Yucatan traded to a certain degree with some of the Caribbean islands, journeying thither in their big dugout canoes.

CHAPTER VIII

THE CALENDAR
(J. E. T.)

The Maya calendar one of the most wonderful products of any nation in the same cultural horizon as the Maya. Lucky and unlucky days and numbers. The calendar was primarily a farmer's almanac. Most of the known Maya glyphs had, probably, some calendaric significance. They were, however, in some cases truly phonetic and often ideographic. The Tzolkin, or sacred year of 260 days. The Maya 365-day year and the named months. The calendar round. Higher periods than the day. The lunar calendar. The Venus calendar. An initial series inscription from Naranjo, with its complete elucidation. Most of the inscriptions on the monuments record even Katun, Lahuntun, and Hotun endings.

THE Maya calendar can rightly be described as one of the greatest, indeed, one might say the greatest, achievement in the line of pure reasoned science ever achieved by a people on the same cultural horizon as the Mayas. It is the concrete result of hundreds of years of patient and acute observation by scientists handicapped by the absence of any scientific instruments, or the mundane rewards too frequently the aim of modern investigators.

Impetus there was, the same impetus that drove Maya civilization upward through the centuries to its greatest heights of art and architecture—love of the soil, and the gods who guarded it. The calendar was primarily devised to show the times when the differ-

PLATE XX.   MAYA DAY SIGNS FROM THE MONUMENTS
After Joyce

ent tasks connected with the agricultural year were due to be commenced. It was, primarily, a farmer's almanac. However, like a modern farmer's almanac, it not only stated bald agricultural facts, it also recorded a great deal of astrology. In the course of time a very elaborate system of lucky and unlucky days grew up. Some day names were lucky, others unlucky, and yet others neither the one nor the other. The same applied to the numbers, which, we shall see, were attached to the day names, as well as the actual months into which the Maya year was divided. With such a basis, permutations of good and bad luck were highly complicated affairs, especially if one also takes into consideration that planets such as Venus and the moon also entered into the computations.

Up to the present time only some 50 per cent of the inscriptions can be translated. However, every glyph, the meaning of which is now known, is either purely calendarical, or denotes some god, ceremony, or idea closely connected with the calendar, and a close examination of the remainder clearly indicates that the vast majority, if not all, fall into the same category.

The Mayas never reached the level of possessing an alphabet. Each word in Maya writing possessed its own glyph, and, as far as we know, verbs in the strict sense of the word could not be written in Maya. Each glyph conveyed its meaning by itself, and stood independent of the rest of the text. The glyphs were mainly ideographic, it would appear. That is they conveyed an idea, and a number of them, although highly conventionalized, plainly reveal this. At the same time a phonetic element enters into many glyphs, as well as that more specialized form of phoneticism known as rebus writing. Students are referred on this point, as indeed on the whole question of hieroglyphs, to Doctor Morley's *An Introduction to the Study of the Maya Hieroglyphs*, more than a brief summary of this fascinating subject being beyond the scope of this book.

The core of the calendar was the sacred year of 260 days, composed of twenty day names (see Plate XX) combined with the numbers 1 to 13. The day names and numbers followed each other without interruption, returning to the beginning at the end of their rounds of 20 and 13 respectively. As the lowest common multiple of these two is 260, the same day name and number could only combine at the end of this period. Below is given a layout of part of this calendar, showing how the 20-day names overlap their numerical attachments.

1	Imix	9	Muluc	4	Caban	12	Chicchan
2	Ik	10	Oc	5	Eznab	13	Cimi
3	Akbal	11	Chuen	6	Cauac	1	Manik
4	Kan	12	Eb	7	Ahau	2	Lamat
5	Chicchan	13	Ben			3	Muluc
6	Cimi	1	Ix	8	Imix	4	Oc
7	Manik	2	Men	9	Ik	5	Chuen
8.	Lamat	3	Cib	10	Akbal		etc.
				11	Kan		

When we say, for example, Thursday, November 21st, we are giving the position of a day first in our seven-day week and then in our year of twelve months. The Mayas did the same thing, if one might compare our seven-day week to their 260-day period. After giving the position of a day in their sacred calendar, or Tzolkin, as it was probably called, they proceeded to give its position in their 365-day year.

This year was divided into eighteen months of twenty days each, making a total of 360 days. To bring the year up to 365 days, they added a special five-day month at the end. This five-day period was considered very unlucky, as explained in Chapter VI.

The names of the months (see Plate XXI) in their order were as follows:

Pop	Mol	Muan
Uo	Chen	Pax
Zip	Yax	Kayab
Zotz	Zac	Cumhu
Tzec	Ceh	Uayeb (5 days only)
Xul	Mac	
Yaxkin	Kankin	

These names, as in the case of the day names, belong to the Yucatecan calendar, invariably used by modern writers. Other Maya tribes in Guatemala and Mexico used different names, though employing the same hieroglyphs as are found on the stelæ and in the codices.

The days of these months were numbered from 0 to

19, with the exception of the final five-day month, the days of which were numbered from 0 to 4. Thus 0 Pop was the first day of the year. 0 Uo followed 19 Pop, and 4 Uayeb was the last day of the year. The Mayas spoke of the first day of the year as 0 Pop because they counted only elapsed time, and the first day would not be called 1 Pop until it was completed. We, too, to a certain extent count only elapsed time, for we speak of 11.30 A.M., whereas we mean we are half way through the twelfth hour. Similarly we do not speak of its being 12 o'clock until the twelfth hour is completed. However, we are not consistent as we speak of the day being the 21st of the month before that day is completed.

This 365-day year ran concurrently with the 260-day year. As there are 105 days more in the former than the latter, the positions of the days of the sacred calendar will be each year 105 positions further advanced, and as five is the highest common factor of the two years, the same combination of day number, day name, month number, and month name can only return after fifty-two years of 365 days. This interval is known as the calendar round, and enables any Maya day within this period to be distinguished from any other.

In order to distinguish one day from another over a longer period and for long calculations, the Mayas made use of a system of reckoning from a mythical re-creation of the world, that fell, according to the correlation followed in this book, in the year 3373 B.C., on a day 4 Ahau that fell on the position 8 Cumhu in the 365-day year.

From this date, 4 Ahau 8 Cumhu, were calculated the number of days that had elapsed to the date which it was wished to commemorate. However, as the day is a clumsy unit with which to calculate over a long space of time, the Mayas devised a series of higher periods, which were the Uinal, Tun, Katun, and Cycle. The day was known as the Kin.

20 Kins made 1 Uinal or 20-day month.

18 Uinals made 1 Tun or year of 360 days.

20 Tuns made 1 Katun or period of 7,200 days.

20 Katuns made 1 Baktun or Cycle of 144,000 days.

There was a still higher period known as a Pictun or Great Cycle. It represented 20 Cycles or Baktuns, and consisted of 2,880,000 days. This represents a period of over 7,000 years, and as it was only used on very rare occasions, it may be ignored by all except advanced students.

The glyphs for these different periods are shown in Plate XXII. In each case there are two different forms, known as the normal and head forms.

The normal sign for the Kin or day is a large St. Andrew's cross enclosed in a cartouche. The head form is the head of Kinich Ahau, the sun god, with his long beard, filed teeth, and square eye.

The normal form of the hieroglyph for the Uinal or twenty-day month is the highly conventionalized full face of the frog. A more realistic, but still very

PLATE XXI. MAYA MONTH SIGNS FROM THE MONUMENTS
After Joyce

conventionalized frog's head in profile is the head form for this period. The head can be recognized by the curl that projects from the back of the mouth and the closed eye.

The head form of the Tun or year is the head of a bird with the usual markings of death or a skeleton. These are a fleshless jawbone and nose and gumless teeth.

The normal form of the Katun or 7,200-day period is the same as the normal form of the Tun glyph, except that above is added a suffix consisting of two conventionalized fish bones one on each side of a small "cauac" sign. The head form is a bird, probably the macaw.

The head form of the Cycle or Baktun, which consists of 144,000 days, is a face with a hand clasped over the jaw. The normal form consists of two "cauac" signs juxtaposed. This "cauac" sign is the main element in a number of glyphs, such as the months Chen, Yax, Zac, and Ceh. With a tail, similar to that of the Kin glyph, it has the meaning of a completed Tun.

Numbers were ordinarily expressed by bars and dots, a bar representing five and a dot one. In this way the number thirteen, for example, was expressed by two bars and three dots. (See Plate XXIV.) Similarly the number nineteen was shown by three bars and four dots. These numerals were written to the left of or above the sign with which they were combined. Zero was shown by a conventionalized flower cut in two, or by an open hand. Often small crescents were employed to preserve the symmetry of an inscription. In the illustration the number six is thus shown with a bar and one dot in the centre flanked by crescents to fill out the blank spaces. These crescents have no numerical significance, and, unfortunately, are a source of great trouble to archæologists, for frequently in eroded inscriptions the dots and crescents are so weathered that it is very difficult to distinguish between them.

Bars and dots, though most frequently used, were not the only means of expressing numbers.

Occasionally heads, each of which has its distinguishing characteristic (see Plate XXIV), are used in place of the ordinary bars and dots. Below are listed the characteristic distinguishing marks of each number:

Zero invariably has a hand over the lower jaw. This is the sign for completion, and is found also in the head form of the cycle glyph.

1 is represented by the head of the moon goddess. The head is youthful with an oblique eye and a two or three-piece forehead ornament.

2 occurs only once in the Old Empire, and the distinguishing mark is not surely known.

3 is characterized by a banded headdress, often with a circular ornament in front as in the illustration.

4 is represented by the head of the sky god with the Roman nose, square eye, and almost toothless mouth. The head of the sky god is used be-

cause he is associated with the four world directions.

5 wears a headdress, which is the Tun sign. He is
Mam, the old old god, associated with the
death of the year during the five odd days that
end it.

6 has a cross symbol in the eye, something like a
hatchet.

7 is distinguished by the peculiar scroll that passes
under the eye and over the bridge of the nose.
The eye is square.

8 is represented by the youthful head of the maize
god with his distinguishing spiral in front of
the forehead.

9 is invariably shown with either a number of dots
or hairs on the chin. Sometimes both dots and
beard are shown.

10 is denoted by the head of the death god with his
bared jawbone, fleshless nose and mouth and
the death markings like percentage signs.

11 is very seldom used in the head form. The
pointed teeth may be the characteristic mark-
ing that denotes this number.

12 is probably distinguished by the peculiar head-
dress, which may represent braided hair.

13 is either shown by a head combining the banded
headdress of three with the bared jawbone of
ten, or by a bird-headed animal with a prominent beak, and teeth and snake's fang pro-

Courtesy of the Field Museum

PLATE XXII. MAYA CALENDARICAL HIEROGLYPHS

1-2. Kim glyph.   3-4. Uinal glyph.   5-6. Tun glyph.   7-8. Katun glyph.
9-10. Cycle (Baktun) glyph.   11. Moon glyph.   12. Venus glyph

jecting from the end of the mouth. This is the head of the god, who presides over the month Zotz.

14 is formed by a combination of the features of the head for four with the bared jawbone characteristic of ten. Indeed from fourteen to nineteen the heads are thus shown combining the fleshless jawbone of ten with the heads of the first digit.

In a few inscriptions the numbers are written by using the whole body. The bodies are, however, purely ornamental, and the clue to the number expressed is to be found in the heads, which are similar to the head numerals already discussed. One of the most beautiful of these inscriptions with full-figure glyphs occupies the back of stela D at Copan, and gives the date 9.15.5.0.0. 8 Ahau 8 Chen.

In addition to carving these elaborate inscriptions, stating the length of time that had elapsed from the date 4 Ahau 8 Cumhu in Baktuns, Katuns, Tuns, Uinals, and Kins, the priest astronomers also made use of a lunar calendar. This was based on observation of the current moon, and was, therefore, liable to a slight error. They stated how many days old the moon was on the day the inscription commemorated, what position it occupied in a five- or six-month period, and whether the current lunar month was of twenty-nine or thirty days, as the Mayas made no use of fractions.

Finally the Mayas made use of a Venus calendar,

based on observation of that planet. Their astronomer priests had realized that the length of the Venus year was 583.92 days, but as they made no use of fractions they corrected the error accumulated by using a 584-day Venus year by dropping four days at the end of every sixty-one Venus years, and eight at the end of every 301 Venus years. This correction was so accurate that had the Venus calendar continued to function uninterruptedly up to the present time, the error over this period of considerably more than a thousand years would not have amounted to more than a day.

Having thus briefly outlined the skeleton of the Maya calendar, let us examine a simple inscription, and translate it glyph by glyph. In Plate XXIII is shown a drawing by Doctor Morley of the opening glyphs of stela 24 at Naranjo. The glyphs are to be read in pairs from left to right. The left column is lettered A, the right column B, and the glyphs from top to bottom are numbered 1 to 7.

A1 is a glyph which stands at the beginning of every Maya inscription of the long count. It gives the name of the god who ruled over the month of the recorded date. In this case the month, to anticipate, is Yax, and this was the month ruled over by the planet Venus, consequently in the first glyph we see as the central element the normal form of glyph for the planet Venus (see Plate XXII).

B1 is the normal form of the cycle glyph with a bar and four dots attached to it. The whole glyph means

nine periods of 400 years have passed. A2 is the glyph
for the Katun with a numerical co-efficient of 12 (note
the oblong in the centre between the two dots. This
is not numerical, but serves solely to balance the carving, and as a concession to the Maya passion for filling
lacunæ). B2 is the normal form of the Tun glyph with
two bars attached, meaning ten years of 360 days each.
A3 is the Uinal glyph with one bar attached, meaning
five months of twenty days. B3 is the Kin, or day sign
with the number twelve, two bars and two dots with an
ornamental oval attached. A4 is the day 4 Eb (notice
the outline of the jawbone, the chief characteristic of
this day sign). There follows in B4 the glyph of the god
who ruled over the night preceding this day. The meaning of the following glyph, that of A5, is unknown, but
in B5 the information is given that this date fell eighteen days after a new moon (note the three bars representing fifteen with the three dots raising the total to
18). A6 states that the current moon was the first in
the series of six, and B6 adds that the current moon was
of twenty-nine days. Finally in A7 the position of this
date in the 365-day year is given as 10 Yax.

Freely translated this inscription then reads: "The
morning star was the patron of the date that is given
below. 3850 years of 360 days have passed since the
date 4 Ahau 8 Cumhu (when the world was recreated?)
and in addition 112 days. The day in our sacred calendar of 260 days is 4 Eb, and in our year of 365 days
the position on which this date falls is 10 Yax. The

PLATE XXIII.   A LONG COUNT DATE
Stela 24 at Naranjo
After Morley

patron god of the night on which this day falls is—. This date is eighteen days after a new moon, and this moon, which is of twenty-nine days, is the first of our lunar cycle of six."

For brevity Maya dates in the long count are written by students in Arabic numbers with the periods omitted, a period or dash separating the different terms, in the same manner as dollars and cents are written with a period separating the dollars from the cents. In this way the initial series given above would be written 9.12.10.5.12. 4 Eb 10 Yax. Similarly the end of the fifteen Katun of cycle nine, for example, is written 9.15.0.0.0., the three zeros denoting that the date is the end of a Katun, and that there are, therefore, no Tuns, Uinals, or Kins.

In actual practice the great majority of the carved dates that have survived are even Katun endings, half Katun endings (called Lahuntuns), as, for example, 9.15.10.0.0., 9.13.10.0.0., etc., or Hotun endings. The Hotun is the five-Tun period, or in other words a quarter Katun, as, for instance, 9.15.5.0.0., or 9.15.15.0.0.

The Mayas, when their civilization was at its height, endeavored to commemorate the passage of every Hotun with a monument. As a rule an inscription opens with the Hotun date the monument was erected to mark. Other dates, that mark important astronomical, or possibly, civil, events, follow. These subsidiary dates are related to the opening date by addition or subtraction. Finally the Hotun, Lahuntun, or Katun

date of erection is repeated at the close of the inscription.

Nevertheless, quite frequently the opening date of
an inscription is not an even Hotun date, but an initial
series recording an uneven number of Tuns, Uinals,
and Kins, as, for instance, the date from Naranjo ex-
amined above. This uneven date is emphasized on this
monument, because the inscription deals with a change
in the method of reckoning moons, and the initial series
of this stela appears to record the date when this change
came into force at Naranjo.

When the opening date on a monument does not
record an even Hotun, the inscription is carried forward by additions to the Hotun that marks the date of
the dedication of the monument. In the case of this
Naranjo stela the dedication of the monument took
place on the date 9.13.10.0.0. 7 Ahau 3 Cumhu. This
was nine Tuns, twelve Uinals, and eight Kins, or
roughly nine and a half of our years later than the
opening date, and this second date in the form of a
calendar round closes the inscription.

The Maya calendar, having no leap year, gradually
crept ahead of the tropical year. This, however, did not
mean that the Maya priest astronomers were ignorant
of the real length of the year. Doctor Teeple has recently discovered that a large number of the initial
series dates that do not record even Hotun endings, are
actually calculations to show the number of days that
the Maya year was ahead of the real year. These cal-

culations show a greater accuracy than that achieved by the Julian calendar, there being an error of only about a couple of days in calculating the length of the tropical year over a period of 3,800 years. These calculations were made by using the coincidences of the moon with the tropical year over long periods. Indeed, in the case of some of the early dates, which were projected over 3,000 years into the past, the age of the moon was given with no error. Although Maya arithmetic may seem cumbersome to us, used as we are to the decimal system, yet it has been surpassed only by the Arabic system for simplicity in handling. Doctor Teeple remarks on the strange fact that in Central America there grew up a civilization, where the wheel and other simple mechanical contrivances and inventions were unknown, but where mathematical knowledge had reached a level unknown in the rest of the world among a primitive race. On the other hand the early cultures of the Old World had discovered the wheel, but had made little progress in mathematics. Strangely among the modern Mayas one sees no evidence of marked mathematical ability, or for that matter artistic ability, which has almost entirely disappeared.

Mistakes in the calculations are by no means rare on the monuments. Many of these mistakes are patent to us, and must have been obvious at the time the monuments were erected. For example there will be, say, an addition of three Uinals and five days to 9.15.0.0.0 4 Ahau 13 Yax. The addition can be easily calculated,

PLATE XXIV. MAYA NUMBERS

Above: Head variants, 0-19. *Below:* "Bar and dot" numerals and thumb variant for 1

After Joyce

and should reach 9.15.0.3.5. 4 Chicchan 18 Mac, but
instead of this date one reads, perhaps 4 Cimi 18 Mac,
an impossible date, first because it is impossible for the
month co-efficient to be 18 when the day sign is Cimi,
and secondly, although 5 Cimi is the day after 4 Chicchan, the day 4 Cimi will not occur till 220 days later,
and then not in association with the month Mac. Sometimes a mistake will occur in the number of days
elapsed since a new moon. Perhaps a bar is added so
that the inscription says that a certain date instead of
being twenty-seven days after a new moon, is thirty-
two days after a new moon, an impossibility, as thirty-
two days after one new moon would be written as two
or three days after the next new moon. Sometimes there
is an error in the sculptured figure. Perhaps a priest or
captive is shown with two left hands, or with both the
feet right feet.

The late Doctor Gordon has suggested that these
mistakes were not accidental, but were made deliberately so that the monument should not be perfect. Certain Oriental peoples have the belief that only the gods
make anything perfect, and, therefore, it would be
something approaching blasphemy for a human being
to produce anything without flaw. He considers that
the Mayas may have had the same idea. On the other
hand, the sculptors, in all probability, had no knowledge of the hieroglyphs they were ordered to carve,
and accordingly may easily have made a mistake. In
that case one might well imagine that the wretched man

paid for his mistake by being offered up as a sacrificial victim in expiation of his error.

Practically all the advance that has been made so far in the decipherment of the hieroglyphs has been with the glyphs connected with the calendar, either directly or indirectly. Little progress, if any, has been made with non-calendarical glyphs. Indeed, it is by no means certain civil events were ever commemorated on the stone monuments, which were, apparently, purely religious and astronomical in character. In any case glyphs that may have had a non-calendarical meaning must, at best, have been very few in number, for although many glyphs have not yet yielded their full meaning, nevertheless in most cases some of the component elements are known to be calendarical. Some of the early Spanish writers speak of hieroglyphic codices devoted to the history of the Mayas. If such did actually exist, there must also have been glyphs to express the names of rulers, cities, lists of tribute paid, and victories gained; however, these were probably employed only in the hieroglyphic codices, and not on the stelæ and altars.

Since the art of writing was first invented, rulers have raised great monuments in commemoration of their deeds and to their own greater glory. Accounts of great victories, lists of booty taken, or records of tribute paid fill the available space—long tales of self-glory. The Mayas, alone of ancient peoples, wrote of scientific matters, substituting abstract mathematical calculations for the empty boastings of vain rulers. In this they were far ahead not only of their contemporaries but also of even our so-called modern civilization.

CHAPTER IX

THE MODERN MAYA
(T. G.)

Extent of the Maya area. Languages spoken. Personal characteristics and physical appearance of the Maya. The work performed by the men and the women. Dress worn by men, women, and children in various parts of the Maya area. The importance of agriculture amongst the Maya. Crops raised. Food and cooking. Traps and other methods used in procuring game. Fire making. House building and the materials used. Frequent changes of sites for their villages. Furniture and household utensils. Pottery making. Spinning and weaving. Villages hidden in the bush. Method of appointing chiefs. Punishments for crimes. Marriage and children. Diseases and medicines. Games. Religion. Curious superstitions. Survivals of their ancient religion. Ceremonies performed to the old gods of agriculture, in which Christian saints are also invoked.

The Maya Indians of To-day.—The modern descendants of the ancient Maya of the Old and New Empires occupy that part of Central America extending between the State of Tabasco on the west, and the Republic of Spanish Honduras on the east.

Throughout the greater part of this area, including the states of Chiapas, Tabasco, Yucatan, Campeche, and Quintana Roo, the Peten district of Guatemala, and British and Spanish Honduras, Maya is spoken, similar to that spoken in the sixteenth century, and presumably differing little from that in use in the Old Empire. In the south of Guatemala, and in Spanish Honduras, a great variety of dialects of Maya are in use, of which the two most important are the Quichè and the Kakchikel.

Personal Characteristics.—Physically, though short, the Maya are robust and well proportioned, the men average five feet two inches in height, the women about two inches less. The skin varies in color from almost pure white to light chocolate. The hair of both sexes is long, black, and coarse on the head, where it grows very low on the forehead, but almost entirely lacking elsewhere.

They, like their forefathers, are an extremely broadheaded people, the cephalic index of a number of Indians from the east coast of Yucatan averaging 88.11. The following indices were obtained from Santa Cruz Indians of pure Maya stock:

Maximum length of head	cm.	17.52
Maximum breadth of head	cm.	15.44
Cephalic index		88.11
Facial height	cm.	11.68
Maximum bi-zygomatic breadth	cm.	12.84
Facial index		84.40
Nasal height	cm.	5.13
Nasal breadth	cm.	3.55
Nasal index		69.30

The eyes are large, and dark brown, the ears small, and closely applied, the nose broad, and the jaw rather prognathous. The teeth are good, though toward middle age they become worn down almost to the gum, from eating corn bread impregnated with grit from stone hand mills. The figure is rather squat, the limbs rounded, and the extremities small and well formed.

The younger women are good looking, even measured by civilized standards. They are both mentally and physically superior to the men, polite and hospitable, though shy with strangers, and very fond of gossip. They are very industrious, rising usually at three or four o'clock in the morning to grind the corn for the day's supply of corn cake. During the day they prepare tobacco, and make cigarettes, gather cotton, which they spin, weave, and embroider for garments. They weave mats of palm leaf and baskets of liana, net hammocks from henequen fibre, and make coarse, domestic pottery ware and incense burners. In addition to these tasks, they look after the children, and do the usual domestic chores.

The men's time is occupied in agriculture, hunting, fishing, and dug-out and house building. They are silent and reserved, though not sullen; civil, obliging, and good-tempered, and take an intelligent interest in everything which touches their own daily lives, but are singularly incurious as to anything going on outside these. They are extraordinarily good bushmen, and possess a faculty, almost amounting to a special sense, for finding their way in the forest.

Both men and women are singularly lacking in sex instinct, and this seems to have been a characteristic of the Maya from the earliest times.

Men and women mix very little; the woman, notwithstanding her superior mentality, is the servant, and always walks a pace or two behind the lord. Terms of endearment, and gestures of affection between the sexes are practically unknown and jealousy can hardly be said to exist.

Dress.—The men wear hats of woven palm leaf, cotton trousers, and short shirt-like jackets hanging outside them.

In some localities they use only the old maxtli, or loincloth, especially when at work in their plantations. In the highlands, particularly during the cold weather, homespun and woven cloaks and woollen garments are worn. They usually wear sandals of tapir hide on their feet, but imported shoes are now beginning to take the place of these.

The women wear two garments of cotton; the huipil, a loose, short-sleeved blouse, cut square at the neck, and falling below the hips, and the pik, or skirt, reaching nearly to the ankles. The edges of these garments are often beautifully embroidered in colors, with human figures, flowers, animals, and geometrical devices.

The smaller children often go naked, but wear a variety of curious objects strung round their necks, small coins, shells, beads, dried seeds, with figurines of stone, wood, pottery and metal. Most of these are worn as charms, or amulets, to protect the wearer from disease, accident, or evil spirits, or to insure good luck.

PLATE XXV.   MAYA INDIAN FEMALE BAND

Agriculture.—The cultivation of his milpa, or corn plantation, is to the Indian the chief business of life, for not only has it, to him, a peculiar religious significance, handed down from countless generations of ancestors, but he knows that if the crop fails, actual starvation will menace his family and himself.

The virgin bush, in which the plantation is made, is cut down in December or January. This is the most arduous part of the work, and the neighbors usually assemble to help each other at it. The felled bush is allowed to dry, and burned over about May, and, after the first shower of rain on the burned area, is planted with corn, by making small holes at regular intervals, in each of which a few grains are dropped. About October, the corn begins to ripen, whereon each stalk is bent on itself, so that the ear hangs down, and rain cannot enter and spoil the grain.

When the corn is ripe it is stored, still in the husk, in little huts in the plantation, and shelled only as required for use. The surplus from that consumed by the family, the pigs, and the dogs—for these also are corn fed—is exchanged at the nearest village for cotton cloth, iron cooking pots, powder and shot, but chiefly for rum.

Many kinds of fruits and vegetables are grown on the plantation, including yams, camotes, squashes, tomatoes, aguacates, sapodilloes, mammy apples, okras, papayas, bread fruit, and a variety of others.

Food and Cooking.—For the first meal of the day they take a hot drink called posol, made of ground corn and water, and often flavored with honey. In the evening the principal meal is eaten, consisting of game, fish, eggs, beans, red pepper, and tortillas, or corn cake, but perhaps more often than not, the menu is confined to the last three items.

Tortillas, all over the Maya area, are, and have been probably for the last 3,000 years, the staple food of the Indian. They are made in the following way. The grain is first soaked, over night, in a lye of wood ashes, to remove the outer husk. The softened grain is then ground into a fine paste, on a slightly concave stone, by means of a stone rolling pin, and during this manipulation the operator literally waters the bread with her sweat, as she bends over her task. When the paste is ready, it is shaped, by hand, into small round, flat cakes, which are baked on an iron or pottery plaque. The woman always does the baking, and hands each tortilla, piping hot, to the man, who eats it. Her turn does not come till he has finished, as they never eat together.

The principal game animals of the district are, the deer, two species of wild hog, gibnut, armadillo, wild turkey, tapir, and curassow.

Communal hunts are often undertaken, and the hunters are very expert at barbecuing the game killed, by smoking the carcasses over a smouldering fire of cedar chips. The meat thus obtained is divided up amongst those participating in the hunt, quite in the ancient Maya way. The bow and arrow have, except in very remote parts, been almost superseded by the muzzle-loader, and even in some cases by the Winchester. The Indian boys, however, are still extraordinarily expert in the use of a leather sling, and usually come in with a load of squirrels and small birds as the result of a day's hunting.

Two varieties of traps are commonly used. For the first, a path frequented by game going to and from a watering place is selected, along this is dug a shallow trench, opposite a springy young sapling. Two stakes are driven in, one on each side of the trench, the one farthest from the sapling having a crook at the top. A piece of cord, with a noose at one end, and with a stick long enough to extend from one stake to the other, firmly tied by its centre above the noose, is attached to the top of the sapling by its other end. The sapling is bent down, and held in place by the stick above the noose, which is grasped lightly between the crook in one stake and the stake opposite it, the loop hanging suspended between the two. Lastly a number of sticks and leaves are scattered lightly over the trench. Animals coming along the run, and putting their heads through the noose, are immediately suspended by the jerking back of the sapling. This trap may be adapted for game of any size, from a tiger to a rabbit.

Another trap, employed only for small animals, consists of an oblong cage of split bamboo, or cabbage palm bark. Over an opening in the top rests an accurately balanced strip of board or bark, baited at one end with corn. When the animal endeavors to reach the bait, it is precipitated into the trap, and the board swings back in place, covering the exit.

Cooking methods are extremely primitive; three large stones are placed at the angles of an equilateral triangle to form the koben, the only fireplace ever used. Between these is kindled the fire of sticks, over which is placed the earthenware pot, or flat disc for baking corn cakes.

Matches are now in common use, but hunters generally make use of dry punk ignited by a flint spark, and in the remote villages fire is still made by rotating a sharp-pointed shaft of some hard wood (usually dogwood) in a hole made in a slab of some very light, dry wood (usually gumbolimbo), round which some fine dry shavings have been scattered.

Both men and women wash their hands before and after each meal, a very necessary procedure, as they eat exclusively with their fingers, using the flexible corn cake as a spoon to scoop up gravy, beans, and other mushy food-stuffs. They eat at small round tables, about sixteen inches high, sitting, or rather squatting, around them on little blocks of wood, four or five inches high. They are very fond of salt, which, near the coast, is often obtained by evaporating sea water, and in the interior, from the ashes of burned botan tops (a species of palm).

Houses are constructed in the following manner. First, a number of straight trees are searched for in the bush; these must be about eight inches in diameter at the base, and crotched on top. Some hard wood, as chi-chem, or Santa Maria, is usually selected. These are then cut down, peeled, and carried to the site of the new house where they are firmly embedded, one at each of the four corners, and others at short intervals along the lines of the wall. Along the crotches, peeled poles, five or six inches in diameter, are laid, and to these are tied still smaller poles, which run up to the ridge pole as rafters. This framework is firmly bound together by ropes of liana. Rows of long thin pliable sticks are next bound round the rafters, and to these are attached layer upon layer of palm leaves, till a thatch, sometimes fifteen inches thick, and quite impervious to rain, is formed.

The walls between the posts are filled in with tasistas, a small species of palm, or with strips of split cabbage palm. The outer sides of the walls may be plastered with adobe, or they may be thatched with palm leaf. Doors and windows are made of a wickerwork of liana, of split cabbage palm, or of a stick frame thatched with palm leaf.

When a man undertakes the building of a new house he calls his friends and neighbors in to help him, and the residence is ready for occupancy in a few days, as all the materials are growing ready to hand in the forest, and require only to be cut down and assembled. The facility with which their houses are constructed, and the difficulty in getting more than one or two crops in succession from each plantation, with their primitive agriculturing methods, probably account for the frequent changes in site which one notices in Indian villages. As the lands in one neighborhood become impoverished, the population has a tendency gradually to desert the old village, and start a new one in a more favorable locality where tracts of still virgin bush exist within convenient reach of the new settlement.

The furniture is of the simplest. A small round cedar table, with a little bowl-shaped projection, which contains red pepper, and salt, at meal times, a few blocks of wood as seats, with perhaps a couple of hollow-backed, solid, wooden armchairs covered with tiger or deer skin, and a number of calabashes, of all shapes and sizes, with earthenware vessels for cooking and holding water. These constitute the usual furnishing of every Maya household.

Hammocks of henequen fibre are hung across the rafters, and if the family is large, are often so close together that navigation in the room is almost impossible at night time.

The Indian's indispensable belongings consist of a hammock, a few calabashes, and pots, a few almuds of corn, a machete, and a cotton suit, all of which he can carry slung over his back in a net, or macapal; with his wife and dogs trotting behind him, he can leave his old home and seek pastures new, with a light heart and untroubled mind, knowing that the bush will provide for all his needs.

Pottery Making.—Pottery making is an art which is

rapidly dying out throughout the Maya area, owing to the introduction of more convenient and durable vessels of metal. It is usually undertaken only by elderly women, who use a fine yellow paste, mixed with sand, or powdered quartz or calabash rind.

A great variety of vessels is manufactured, their chief uses being for the storage of water, or dry materials, as beans, rice or corn, and as cooking pots. The Indian potters do not use the wheel, though occasionally a sort of turntable is employed. The smaller vessels are moulded by hand, and the larger built up by coiling ribbons of wet clay one above the other, the junctions being smoothed off with a little spade-shaped wooden implement.

Neither glaze, paint, nor polish is applied to the pottery; the only decoration used being a series of depressions round the rim. The ware is burned in a clear open charcoal fire. In some parts of the Maya area, the Indians still manufacture their ancient censers, used in the worship of the old gods, displaying the face or full figure of the god on the outside, but these are now extremely crude, and the face is often represented solely by two ear plugs, a dab of clay for the nose, and a slit for the mouth.

Spinning and Weaving.—A spindle of hard, heavy wood is used, weighted about three inches from the bottom with a ring of pottery or hard-wood. The upper end of this is turned rapidly between the right finger and thumb, and the lower revolved in a small bowl, or shallow calabash. The cotton may be held in the left hand, or placed upon the shoulder.

The loom is a very simple affair, consisting of a cloth and yarn beam of light wood.

The cloth beam is attached to the weaver's chest by a cord passing round his back, enabling him to tighten the warp by simply leaning backward. The yarn beam is generally attached to a doorpost. The shuttle consists of a light stick, pointed at both ends, on which the weft is wound obliquely. All the alternate warp strands may be lifted together by means of a heddle, consisting of a number of loops attached to a rod, each loop passing round a warp strand, so that when the rod is raised the warp threads are raised with it. The lease rods consist of splints of heavy wood, usually sapote, two to three inches broad, and one-third of an inch thick in the centre, with sharp edges and pointed ends.

The loom used for cotton cloth rarely exceeds two feet in breadth.

Baskets are woven from liana, and from split cane. The liana ones are usually very large, and used only for carrying corn in from the plantation, the cane ones are finer and smaller, and used for all sorts of domestic purposes.

Henequen fibre, manufactured from the leaves of the American aloe, by placing them on a flat board, running water over them, and then scraping away the pulp with a flat grooved stone, is used in the manufacture of rope, cord, hammocks, and rough cloth.

PLATE XXVI.   LUBAANTUN

Kechi girls hulling rice in wooden mortars

Candles are made by dipping cotton thread in black wax, produced by the native bee, and oil for burning in small earthenware lamps, from cuhoon nut kernels.

Villages.—These vary in size from two or three houses to 100 or more. In the smaller villages, the houses are placed quite irregularly. In the larger, they usually form more or less regular streets, surrounding a central plaza containing the church and dance house.

Each house is surrounded by its own enclosed yard, in one part of which the bush is allowed to grow high, to afford a convenient latrine for the women.

Dogs, pigs, and vultures serve as scavengers.

The villages are surrounded by a maze of paths, which make it very difficult for a stranger to find them without a guide, and the Indians take the greatest pains to conceal their settlements, even going so far, in some cases, as to cut out the tongues of their cocks, so that their crowing shall not betray the site.

On the death of a head chief, amongst the Icaiche and Santa Cruz Indians, the oldest sub-chief is supposed to succeed him, but as a matter of fact there are always rival claimants, and the sub-chief with the strongest personality, the largest following amongst the soldiers, usually grasps the office. The sub-chiefs are elected by the people. The power of the head chief is absolute over the whole trible, but it is rarely that he dies a natural death.

Imprisonment is unknown amongst the Indians, fine, flogging, and death being the only punishments inflicted. Fines and flogging may be administered by the sub-chiefs, death, only by the head chief. The severity of the flogging and amount of the fine are regulated by the nature of the offence.

To carry out the death sentence, three or four soldiers are chosen, who chop the victim over the head with their machetes, preferably when they catch him asleep, or off his guard. Several men always act together as executioners, in order that no single individual may be held responsible for the killing, and start a feud with the victim's relatives.

Marriage and Children.—Formerly the Indian girls did not marry till they reached the age of thirteen and fourteen years; now, they often marry at twelve, and whereas before, the first question of his prospective father-in-law to a young man, was, "How many mecates of corn and cotton have you?" now, owing to the shortage of men, the father is only too glad to get a husband of any kind for his daughter. The marriage ceremony among the Santa Cruz is performed by an official called the Yumxrib, whose office is somewhat analogous to that of Colonial Secretary in a British Colony.

The marriage tie is not very binding. If the father and mother separate, the younger children remain with the latter; of the older children, the father takes the boys, the mother the girls. If small children are left destitute by the death of both parents, the nearest relative takes them, or, in the absence of relatives, they are distributed by the sub-chief amongst families of his choosing in their own village.

Diseases and Medicines.—The Indian's hold on life is a loose one, and easily detached. An elderly man without any apparent physical symptoms, except anæmia and enlarged spleen, from which all suffer, will suddenly take to his hammock and announce to friends and relatives. "He in cimil, I am going to die," whereupon he wraps himself in a sheet, refuses food and drink, turns his face to the wall, and does die, apparently from sheer disinclination to live.

Malaria, with enlarged spleen, and hookworm are the commonest disease amongst the Indians. For malaria, a sudorific made by boiling the leaves of the sisim tree in water is used, the patient lying wrapped in a blanket, in his hammock, with a fire underneath, to help the action of the drug.

This treatment is successful, but unfortunately the patient, after he begins to sweat, often plunges into cold water, and takes a severe chill, more dangerous than the fever.

Smallpox, when it visits an Indian village, is a terrible scourge, as the native has not acquired the partial immunity of a civilized community. Sometimes the whole population of a village will depart en masse, leaving the dead unburied, and the stricken lying in their hammocks, with a supply of food and drink beside them, to do the best they can.

Venereal diseases are rare amongst the Maya, and

syphilis is practically unknown; indeed, they seem to be immune to the attacks of this disease. It has been suggested that this partial immunity was acquired owing to the fact that the disease had been prevalent in the New World long before the Conquest, and that it was originally brought from the New World to the Old, and not vice versa.

Simple fractures are set very successfully by getting the fractured ends in apposition by extension, surrounding the seat of fracture with a layer of cotton wool, and applying over this, round the whole limb, a series of small wooden splints, over which a henequen cord is wound to keep the whole in apposition. Excellent results are obtained in this way.

Bleeding is one of the favorite remedies of the native doctor. Blood is usually let from the temporal vein, but sometimes from the forearm. A chip of obsidian, a sharp splinter of bone, or a snake's tooth serves as lancet. The last, though the least efficient as a lancet, is most frequently used, as it is credited with certain thaumaturgic powers.

A great variety of native plants is used by the Maya for medicinal purposes, some of which are purely empirical, others produce definite physiological results, and are often used with good effect, while a third class is administered, apparently, on the assumption that "similia similibus curantur," because of some resemblance in the form of the plant to the diseased part.

Decoctions made from the charred carcasses of animals were at one time very popular, as remedies for various diseases, each malady yielding to some specific animal, though the connection between the remedy and the disease was difficult to trace.

Eye troubles are treated by placing a small seed, for twenty-four hours, beneath the lower lid. On withdrawing the seed, it is naturally covered with a layer of mucus, to which the doctor points as the injurious matter, the cause of the trouble, which he has successfully removed.

In parturition, the dorsal position, upon the floor, is usual. Vigorous massage is carried out by the midwife, especially over the uterus. If this fails, the patient is made to vomit, by pushing a coil of her own hair down her throat, and failing this, a woman of exceptional lung power blows into her open mouth; all obviously methods of applying the "vis a tergo," where "vis a fronte" is not applicable.

Games.—Many games are played by both children and adults, but most of these have probably been introduced from Europe.

Tak-in-kul, however, one of their favorites, is probably indigenous. In this a number of players stand in a row, their hands behind their backs. One player stands in front of the row, and one, who holds a disc of pottery in his hands, behind. The disc-holder places it in the hand of one of those in the line, who passes it to his neighbor, keeping it in constant circulation up and down the line. The player in front has to guess in whose hand the disc is at the moment of guessing. If he is right, he joins the line, and the holder of the disc takes his place. This is a lively game, and often used as a medium for gambling.

Chac is played with pottery discs, which are tossed from the palm to the back of the hand. The player who drops fewest discs in a given number of throws wins.

The boys make little bows, and arrows tipped with black wax, with which they play war and hunting games. They also make bull roarers from large dry seed pods, and spinning tops from cuhoon nuts, with hardwood spikes inserted in the base, and they are very expert in the use of the sling.

Most of their games have European prototypes, and are probably imported, as certainly are the modified forms of cricket, football, and baseball played by the youth of many of the villages and most closely in contact with civilized communities.

Religion.—Many curious superstitions are current amongst the Maya. They believe that the air is full of the souls of the dead, called "Pishan," who are at liberty at all times to return to earth, and at certain seasons are compelled to do so.

They are able to enjoy the spirit of food, drink, and other refreshment set out for them, but not the substance. Some are good and some evil, some friendly, and others inimical to mortals.

They also believe in beings called Xtabai, who, although they have never lived on earth as mortals, are able to assume human form. These are invariably evil, and enemies of the human race. They usually take the form of beautiful women, who lie in wait for travellers and entice them into the forest, where they disappear, and are never again heard of.

They believe firmly in a future existence, where good and evil done in this life are respectively rewarded and punished. Their conception of heaven, however, approaches nearer the Mohammedan than the Christian ideal, and is perhaps a mixture of the two, the material part being derived from their ancient religion. The houri enters little, if at all, into their conception of bliss, for the Maya is extraordinarily deficient in sex feeling.

The connection between this world and the next is regarded as rather close, and an Indian will whisper a message for a dead friend into the ear of a newly deceased corpse, in the confident belief that it will be delivered with promptness and dispatch.

Numbers of clay images, most of them attached to incense burners, are found all over the Maya area, in caves, and around and in ancient burial mounds. These, the Indians believe, are, at certain seasons, endowed with life, and live and move, dance, eat, and drink just like mortals. These images are nearly all those of their ancient gods, and on this account they are very loth to remove them from where they are found, and indeed not infrequently make offerings of flowers, and burn candles before them.

They believe that the Christian saints also can be persuaded sometimes, if importuned insistently, to return to earth and perform acts of grace for their devotees, but whereas their own gods are usually mischievous, and often malignant in their actions, the saints are invariably beneficent and helpful.

Professedly they are Christians, but the longer one lives amongst them, and the better one gets to know them, the more one realizes that their Christianity is, to a great extent, merely a thin veneer, that fundamentally their religious conceptions, and especially their ritual and ceremonies, are survivals—degenerate, much changed, and with most of their significance lost—of those of their ancestors.

To Christianity, not as a new and separate religion, but as an extension and amplification of the one they already practised, they seem to have taken kindly from the first, and this attitude seems to have been rather fostered and encouraged by the missionary fathers, those zealous apostles who sought souls as eagerly as the conquerors sought gold.

This attitude toward Christianity was almost unavoidable, when one considers the really extraordinary resemblances which exist between the two religions, both in doctrine and ritual.

At the present day the Sun god, the Wind god, the Rain god, St. Laurence, Santa Clara, and the Virgin, may all be invoked in the same prayer, and the cross is substituted, in most of the ceremonies, for the images of the old gods, though the latter are still invoked by name. The four principal ceremonies of the Indians are, as might be expected, closely associated with agriculture, and particularly with the corn crop.

The first of these takes place at the cutting of the bush in which the corn plantation is to be made, the second at the planting of the corn, the third during its ripening, and the fourth at harvest time.

There is a close resemblance, at all these ceremonies, between the prayers and offerings made to the gods, but the third, known as the Cha Chaac, which takes place during the ripening of the corn, and the object of which is to secure sufficient rain for that purpose, is by far the most important, and deserves a somewhat detailed description.

The day before the ceremony, the men dug a large oblong hole in the ground, known as a "pib," to serve as an oven, and erected two palm-leaf huts, in a clearing made in the bush. In one of these an altar was erected, arched over by boughs of sacred Jabin leaves. The women meanwhile were busy preparing great quantities of ground corn, pumpkin seeds, and beans.

On the day of the ceremony, the priest, a little wizened long-haired Indian, dressed in clean white cotton, turned up early in the morning. He was called indifferently by the title "Men," "Chac," or "Ahkin," all terms used before the conquest to designate various grades in the priesthood.

The ceremony was opened by the making of cakes

from corn paste, calabash seeds, and balchè—the native fermented drink—every participant adding his own portion of corn paste to each cake. These were then wrapped in palm-leaf sheaths, ready for the oven. The pib was next heated, by having a great fire kindled within it, in which large stones were made red hot.

Next, fowls and turkeys were brought before the altar, and held by an assistant, while the priest poured balchè down their throats, and dedicated them to the gods, after which they were killed. All the food offerings, wrapped in palm leaves, were next placed on the red-hot stones, at the bottom of the pib, and covered with the earth which had been dug out to make it. While the food was baking, a great variety of corn drinks was placed upon the altar, with jars of balchè, and corn-husk cigarettes, and dedicated to the gods.

The pib was next opened, by having the earth removed from it, and the steaming food offerings, in their palm-leaf wrappers, removed, and placed upon the altar.

All the food and drink offerings were next presented to the gods, a small portion of each being scattered to each of the four cardinal points by the priest, who recited, while doing so, the following prayer, in Maya:

"Now my beautiful lady of the yellow-leaf breadnut, as well as you my handsome father San Isidro, tiller of the earth, as well as you lord Sun, who are seated at the east, as well as you Chanttupchaac who are seated in the middle of the heavens in the east, as well as you Yumcanchaacoob; I deliver to you, with the majestic servants in the middle of the heavens. As well as you my handsome father Ahcanankakabool, as well as you my handsome father Cakael Uxmaal, as well as you my beautiful lady Santa Clara, as well as you my handsome father Xualakmik, as well as you my beautiful lady Xhelik, as well as you my handsome father San Lorenzo, as well as you my beautiful lady of Guadelupe, as well as you Lord Mosonikoob that blows within the milpa when it burns. I deliver then to you this Holy Grace, that you may taste it, and because you are the greatest saints on earth. This is all, my master. Pardon my sins, you have not to follow the holy souls, because I have made this offering."

After this, everything, food, drink, and tobacco, was consumed, to the last morsel and drop, by the participants, and lastly all the materials used in the ceremony was completely destroyed by being burned, so that nothing used in the service of the gods should be contaminated by mortal use.

It is regarded as most important that everything used in the ceremony should be fresh and new. The calabashes must never have been used before, the corn drinks and food must be freshly made and cooked, the living sacrifices, fowls, turkeys, or curassow, must be freshly killed, the huts and altar must be made for the occasion from material newly cut in the bush, in fact the two essentials to success are freshly prepared material, and its complete consumption after the ceremony is finished.

BIBLIOGRAPHY

A complete bibliography of the Maya civilization would occupy many pages, but below are listed a few of the important publications on the subject that should prove of interest to the general reader. Those marked with an asterisk are of a general nature and not technical. For a fuller bibliography see Doctor Morley's "The Inscriptions at Copan."

Blom, F., and La Farge, O.—*Tribes and Temples.* Department of Middle American Research, Tulane University. New Orleans, La., 1927.

Bowditch, C. P.—*The Numeration, Calendar Systems, and Astronomical Knowledge of the Mayas.* Cambridge, Mass., 1910.

Brinton, D. G.—*The Maya Chronicles.* Library of American Aboriginal Literature, vol. I. Philadelphia, 1882.

Cogolludo, D. L.—*Historia de Yucatan.* Merida, 1867–68.

Gann, T. W. F.—*The Maya Indians of Southern Yucatan and Northern British Honduras.* Bureau of American Ethnology, Bulletin 64. Washington, 1916.

In an Unknown Land. New York (Scribners) and London (Duckworth), 1924.

Mystery Cities. New York (Scribners) and London (Duckworth), 1925.

Ancient Cities and Modern Tribes. New York (Scribners) and London (Duckworth), 1926.

Maya Cities. New York (Scribners) and London (Duckworth), 1927.

Discoveries and Adventures in Central America. New York (Scribners) and London (Duckworth), 1928.

Holmes, W. H.—*Archæological Studies among the Ancient Cities of Mexico.* Field Museum, Anthropological Series, vol. I. Chicago, 1895–97.

BIBLIOGRAPHY

Joyce, T. A.—*Mexican Archæology.* London (Lee Warner), 1914.

    Guide to the Maudslay Collection. British Museum. London, 1923.

    Maya and Mexican Art. London (The Studio), 1927.

Landa, Diego de.—*Relacion de las cosas de Yucatan.* Edited and with French translation by Jean Genet. Paris, 1928.

Maler, T.—*Researches in the Central Portion of the Usamacintla Valley.* Memoirs of the Peabody Museum, vol. II, nos. 1 and 2. Cambridge, Mass., 1901 and 1903.

    Explorations of the Upper Usamacintla and Adjacent Region. Ibid., vol. IV, no. 1, 1908.

    Explorations in the Department of Peten, Guatemala, and Adjacent Region. Ibid., vol. IV, nos. 2 and 3, 1908 and 1910.

    Explorations in the Department of Peten, Tikal. Ibid., vol. V, no. 1, 1911.

Maudslay, A. P.—*Biologia Centrali Americana.* Four volumes of plates and one volume of text. London (Bernard Quaritch), 1902.

    A Glimpse at Guatemala. (In collaboration with Mrs. Maudslay.) London, 1899.

Morley, S. G.—*Introduction to the Study of Maya Hieroglyphs.* Bureau of American Ethnology, Bulletin 57. Washington, D. C., 1915.

    The Inscriptions at Copan. Carnegie Institution, Publication no. 219. Washington, D. C., 1920.

Spinden, H. J.—*A Study of Maya Art.* Memoirs of the Peabody Museum, vol. VI. Cambridge, Mass., 1913.

    Ancient Civilizations of Mexico and Central America. American Museum of Natural History, Handbook Series no. 3. New York, 1922.

    Reduction of Maya Dates. Papers of the Peabody Museum of American Archæology and Ethnology, vol. VI, no. 4. Cambridge, Mass., 1926.

Stephens, J. L.—*Central America, Chiapas, and Yucatan.* New York, 1841.

    Incidents of Travel in Yucatan. New York, 1843.

Thompson, J. E.—*A Correlation of the Mayan and European Calendars.* Field Museum of Natural History, Anthropological Series, vol. XVII, no. 1. Chicago, Ill., 1927.

*The Civilization of the Mayas. Field Museum of Natural History, Anthropology Leaflet 25. Chicago, Ill., 1927.

Las comunicaciones y comercio de los antiguos Mayas. Anales de la Sociedad de Geografia e Historia, vol. VI, no. 1. Guatemala, 1929.

Ethnology of the Mayas of Central and Southern British Honduras. Field Museum of Natural History, Anthropological Series, vol. XVII, no. 2. Chicago, Ill., 1930.

Tozzer, A. M.—A Comparative Study of the Maya and Lacondones. New York, 1907.

Villacorta, A., and Rodas, F.—Manuscrito de Chichicastenango (Popol Buj). Guatemala, 1928.

INDEX

Macaw, 190

Maize, developed by Maya, 9, 10; staff of life of Maya, 32, 185, 186

Mams, the, 156

Mani, 64, 86; Chilam Balaam of, 74

Marriages, of Maya, 170–172

Maya, the, short heads, 4; evidence of communication between Toltecs and, 5; origin of, 8, 9; agriculturalists, 9, 12, 65, 120 ff., 187–189, 204, 233; migration of, 11, 29 ff., 60, 71, 79, 85; Morley believes originally nomadic tribe, 12; sources of information concerning, 12 ff.; destruction of literature of, 14, 15; codices of, 14–16; discovery of cotton fabric of, 16; historical records of, 16, 17; three principal clans of, 18; chronological system of, 21–23; religion of, 24–28, 65, 118 ff.; never completely subjugated, 28, 97; human sacrifice among, 35, 93, 131 ff.; cities founded by, 36 ff.; three historical epochs recognized by, 48; New and Old Empires of, 53; possibility of confederation of Old Empire cities, 58; complete abandonment of Old Empire, 60 ff.; possible original, 68; Yucatecan, 72; Mopan, 86; diseases and medicines of, 88, 95, 245–247; slaves, 95, 177; British friends of, 96, 97; architecture of, 98 ff.; art of, 104 ff.; pottery of, 109–112; religious ceremonies of, 139–155, 169, 170; myths and legends, 155–164; horoscope cast, 166; skull deformation, artificial production of squint, and depilation, 166, 167; education, 170; drunkenness, 147, 155, 172, 185; method of punishing, 170, 243, 244; marriages among, 170–172, 244; mourning the dead, and burial customs, 172–174; belief in future life, 173, 249; laws of inheritance, 174, 177; games of, 177, 178, 247, 248; warfare among, 178 ff.; dances of, 183; music, 184; clothing and ornaments, 193 ff.; tattooing, 195;

hairdressing, 196; calendar of, 204–226; languages, 227; modern, area occupied by, 227; appearance and characteristics, 228–230; dress of, 230; food and cooking, 233 ff.; move homes frequently, 237, 238

Mayapan, 82, 149; League of, 18, 83; destruction of, 84, 85; houses in, 196

Mecate, 187

Mens, 26

Merchants, Maya, 200, 201

Mercury, found at Copan, 114

Merida, 94, 96, 179

Metals, found in Maya area, 114, 115

Metnal, 129

Mexico, development of aborigines revealed in stratification of, 4–6; influence of, in Yucatan, 81, 83, 136, 137; mercenaries from, 82, 84, 87; game played in, 177; stones imported from, 201

Migration, of aboriginals to America, 4; of Maya hill tribes, 10, 11; of Maya, 29 ff., 60, 71, 79, 85

Minerals, 201

Monjas, the, 100

Monolith, largest sculptured Mayan, 51

Montejo, Francisco, 92, 93

Months, Maya, 143, 144, 149, 208

Monuments, *see* Stelæ

Moon, 127; time calculated by, 221, 222

Morley, Doctor, 12, 57, 207, 217

Mouldings, stucco, 47, 59

Music, of the Maya, 184

Nacon, 182

Nacons, the, 130, 152

Nahua tribes, 63

Ñakum, 50

Naranjo, stela at, 217, 221

New Year, Maya, 143–147

Nicaragua, 53

Numbers, means of expressing, 212 ff.

Obsidian, 201